Cambridge Elements ☰

Elements in Second Lan[...]
edited b[...]
Alessandro [...]
The University of [...]
John W. Schw[...]
Wilfrid Laurier University, Ontario

T0277524

FOCUS ON FORM

Alessandro Benati
The University of Hong Kong

CAMBRIDGE
UNIVERSITY PRESS

CAMBRIDGE
UNIVERSITY PRESS

University Printing House, Cambridge CB2 8BS, United Kingdom

One Liberty Plaza, 20th Floor, New York, NY 10006, USA

477 Williamstown Road, Port Melbourne, VIC 3207, Australia

314–321, 3rd Floor, Plot 3, Splendor Forum, Jasola District Centre,
New Delhi – 110025, India

79 Anson Road, #06–04/06, Singapore 079906

Cambridge University Press is part of the University of Cambridge.

It furthers the University's mission by disseminating knowledge in the pursuit of
education, learning, and research at the highest international levels of excellence.

www.cambridge.org
Information on this title: www.cambridge.org/9781108708340
DOI: 10.1017/9781108762656

© Alessandro Benati 2021

First published 2021

A catalogue record for this publication is available from the British Library.

ISBN 978-1-108-70834-0 Paperback
ISSN 2517-7974 (online)
ISSN 2517-7966 (print)

Focus on Form

Elements in Second Language Acquisition

DOI: 10.1017/9781108762656
First published online: April 2021

Alessandro Benati
The University of Hong Kong

Author for correspondence: Alessandro Benati, agbenati58@gmail.com

Abstract: This Cambridge Element examines the role and nature of focus on form in second language acquisition. An overall assessment of the role of instruction and the nature of language is provided. Instruction might have a facilitative role in the rate of acquisition. The Element briefly reviews empirical research examining the relative effects of different types of *focus on form* and presents some of the key implications for second language learning and teaching. An effective *focus-on-form* type is one that is input and meaning oriented. Manipulating input to facilitate language processing and form–meaning connections might enhance second language acquisition.

Keywords: focus on form, explicit knowledge, explicit knowledge, language, instruction

ISBNs: 9781108708340 (PB), 9781108762656 (OC)
ISSNs: 2517-7974 (online), 2517-7966 (print)

Contents

1 Introduction

1.1 What Is This Element About?

This Element will analyse and describe the role, nature, and effects of focus on form in second language acquisition theory and research. Focus on form is a term which has been sometimes used to express different meanings. Long (1991) made a clear distinction between 'focus on form' and 'focus on forms' in language instruction. Focus on forms is a term used to describe a type of pedagogical intervention that focuses on the explicit teaching of specific linguistic forms (one at the time) in a target language (e.g. discrete-point grammar presentation and practice). Focus on form can be described as involving a focus on meaning and a focus on form. During focus on form, L2 learners' attention is being focused on specific linguistic properties of the target language in the course of a communicative activity. More broadly 'focus on form' can be described as any pedagogical intervention aiming at drawing L2 learners' attention to the linguistic properties of a language through exposure to meaningful input. In this Element, research, theory, and pedagogy related to different types of 'focus on form' will be presented and discussed. Implications of research on 'focus on form' will be highlighted at the end of this Element. However, before we begin, a general definition of the nature and role of language and instruction is needed.

1.2 What Is the Nature of Language?

There is a considerable debate over the nature and design of the internal mechanisms that create our so-called internal language system (so-called mental representation). There are two competing accounts (domain-general and language-specific) on the nature of language in the field, as highlighted by Keating (2018). One account about the nature of language argues that language is like any other complex mental tasks such as reading, playing chess, and in general solving problems. Like any other complex mental phenomena, it is learned via the same domain-general mechanisms that enable us to learn how to program a computer or solve difficult puzzles. A second account instead, contends that language is special and it is not learned in the same way as other complex mental phenomenon. Their claim is that humans are hardwired to learn language and have cognitive mechanisms specifically designed to deal with language. These are separate mechanisms from the domain-general one.

Regardless of scholars' approach to language, there is a general agreement that language is complex, abstract, and implicit. Each human being creates an internal language system we call language, no matter whether it is a first, second or third language. This abstract and complex system is also implicit in nature, as we know we have language in our heads, but we do not really know what the contents of this language system are.

Language can be described as multi-componential as it comprises of a lexicon, syntax, phonology, and other systems (VanPatten, 2016). Much of the grammatical information is stored in lexical entries with embedded features. What every speaker/knower of language creates in the mind/brain is an implicit, abstract representation of language. What we observe as 'language' is the result of a complex interaction of principles, constraints, and interfaces that yield utterances/sentences.

Language is implicit in nature and abstract as its features are difficult to describe with exact words. It includes what it is allowed (e.g. *Do you know how to get to the centre?*), but it also includes what it is not allowed in a specific language (e.g. *Know how to get to the centre?*). Language does not consist of rules in the classic sense as argued by VanPatten (2010). However, as argued by VanPatten and Benati (2010), a good deal of second language acquisition research talks about the learning of rules and the testing of rules (e.g. learning the passive rule, learning rules for the subjunctive, etc.). The surface phenomena we talk about as 'rules' are real, but what exists in the mental representation are not these rules. What language learners have in their heads are not rules but an abstract system consisting of features and operations plus operations on how those operation can happen.

Language as mental representation is characterized by principles that are universal. These principles constrain the development of language. For example, all languages have a basic structural feature called 'phrase'. This basic feature consists of two elements: head and compliment. Depending on the specific language, we can have 'head first' or 'head final'. English is head first (head + compliment) whereas Japanese is head final (compliment + head) for instance. These abstract notions interact with input language. In addition, language learners possess a complex network of form–meaning connections which evolves and expands establishing lexical and formal relationships as they are exposed to more meaningful and comprehensible input. Language learners have a vast interconnected network of words which encode both meaning and grammatical information. Connections develop in our head not through practice, but through consistent exposure to input. Language is processed and acquired not through pedagogical rules (shorthand ways to describe things that are generally not describable) but through exposure to meaningful input (language that contains a message and L2 learners must attend to the input to process meaning). There is also an important distinction to make between language as mental representation (the internal, abstract, and implicit language system) and language as skill (the accuracy and fluency in language use). Skill can be defined as the ability to use language in real time (speaking, writing, listening and reading), and it involves the intersection of accuracy and fluency (speed in using the target language) (DeKeyser, 2015). Language learners normally acquire skills by participating in skill-based activities. Accuracy refers to how language learners can produce language error-free. Fluency instead, refers to how (speed and confidence) language learners can perform an activity (Housen and Kuiken, 2009).

1.3 Does Instruction Make a Difference?

This was the question originally raised in Long's (1983) seminal paper. Since then, the debate about the role of instruction has focused on whether instruction makes a difference in the acquisition of morphosyntactic properties. Contemporary theories (see VanPatten and Benati, 2010) have also addressed this question by taking different positions around the nature, role, and effects of instruction, particularly in relation to language as representation.

An overall review of the main contemporary theories and current empirical research on the role of instruction in second language acquisition has led to the following conclusions:

- Instruction does not alter the route of acquisition (i.e. acquisition orders and developmental sequences). There are no empirical studies showing that instruction alters the order/sequence of acquisition (Pienemann and Lenzing, 2015);
- Instruction as input manipulation can facilitate language processing. Input manipulation refers to how language can be restructured so that L2 learners can be exposed to grammatical properties of a target language;
- Instruction may have some beneficial effects – for example, developing procedural knowledge (how to do something in a language) or facilitating noticing and awareness – on second language acquisition. Awareness can be defined as learners' degree of consciousness in learning a language. Noticing refers to the ability for L2 learners to notice certain linguistic elements in the input.

The effects of instruction are limited and constrained by natural orders of acquisition and by L2 learners' readiness to acquire a particular structure (Pienemann and Lenzing, 2015). If, as it seems to be the case, there are no effects on instruction on the route of acquisition, what about its possible effects on the rate of acquisition? Can instruction facilitate and speed-up acquisition of the formal properties of a target language?

The effects of a number of different instructional treatments (e.g. incidental focus on form, input enhancement, processing instruction, interactional and corrective feedback, output, and collaborative tasks) have been investigated. Overall, the main findings from the empirical research conducted seem to point to two main positions: (i) instruction has a limited and constrained role; and (ii) instruction might have some possible beneficial effects, not on the route but on the rate of acquisition. However, several key questions (VanPatten, Smith and Benati, 2019) have been raised about how the possible effects of instruction are measured in second language research. Does the research on the effects of instruction measure explicit knowledge or implicit knowledge? In other words, the question is whether empirical research on the effects of instruction measure knowledge about language (i.e. textbook rules) or language as a mental representation.

Very often, the effectiveness of a particular instructional treatment has been measured using explicit knowledge tests. These kinds of tests normal measure knowledge and use of rules that we find in textbooks, teacher explanations, and online sites.

Current research on the effects of instruction has mainly focused on measuring its immediate effects using various designs (VanPatten, Smith and Benati, 2019). It is not clear that instruction on formal features of language speeds up the rate of acquisition. However, there is some evidence that instruction as input manipulation can facilitate language processing (VanPatten, Smith and Benati, 2019). In addition, instruction may have some beneficial effects (e.g. developing procedural knowledge, facilitating noticing and awareness) on second language acquisition. Despite this, there is no enough evidence to demonstrate long-terms effects for instruction. Meta-analysis studies point to positive short-term effects for instruction on grammatical properties of language (Go et al., 2015; Kang, Sok and ZhaoHong, 2019; Norris and Ortega, 2000: Spada and Tomita, 2010) indicate that there is a possible short-term effect of instruction on L2 learners' rate of acquisition. However, the results from these meta-analysis studies need to be taken with caution for two main reasons:

- The effects of instruction measured on the rate of acquisition is mostly about the development of explicit knowledge;
- Measurements in research on the effects of instruction make use of tests that exclusively measure explicit knowledge.

One key question that needs to be addressed is therefore: Does instruction foster implicit knowledge?

1.4 Does Instruction Foster Implicit Knowledge?

There is agreement in second language acquisition that there are two different types of linguistic knowledge: explicit knowledge and implicit knowledge.

Krashen (1982) distinguished between a learning system (explicit) and an acquiring system (implicit). The existence of a difference between implicit and explicit language knowledge is confirmed by brain science. Paradis (2004) sustains that explicit knowledge (conscious awareness of language data) is qualitatively different from implicit knowledge (unconscious set of computational procedures). According to Paradis (2004), explicit rules in grammar do not correspond to the internal and implicit mental representations our mind/brain relies on for language development.

Explicit knowledge of language is defined as conscious knowledge. It is often verbalizable knowledge about language such as 'to talk about something in the past, add *-ed* sound to the end of the verb such as *play* versus *played*'. Implicit knowledge is defined as unconscious knowledge and it is not verbalizable. It is the ability to understand or supply *talked* and not *talk* in contexts that require the past tense in English, and to do so without a conscious effort to retrieve the form.

In traditional instruction, language teachers instruct learners about something, L2 learners practice it, and then the teachers assess them using a paper-and-pencil test. There are two problems with this type instruction aiming at developing explicit knowledge: (i) it does not correspond to the way language develops in the mind/brain; (ii) it does not correspond to the way learners process information.

Language acquisition is about the development of implicit knowledge. As highlighted VanPatten and Rothman (2014), language as mental representation is too abstract and complex to be taught and learned explicitly. In short, language is not the rules and paradigms that appear on textbook pages. Explicit rules and paradigm lists cannot become the abstract and complex system because the two things are completely different. This implication stems from the fact that there is no internal mechanism (at least no strong evidence for one) that can convert explicit textbook rules into implicit mental representation (VanPatten, 2016).

Instruction has an effect on fostering explicit knowledge, at least in the short-term. DeKeyser (2015) argues that practice in which learners deliberately focus their attention on particular forms might help the development of a skill. Practice of the kind used in traditional instruction does little to foster the development of mental representation and might help the development of a learning-like behaviour. VanPatten and Benati (2010: 31) have argued that 'L2 learners clearly create linguistic systems in an organized way that seem[s] little affected by external forces such as instruction and correction'.

The acquisition of the grammatical properties of a target language is mainly implicit. L2 learners create an abstract system (mental representation) similar to the way in which L1 learners do. Therefore, instruction should be devised in a way that, on one hand, enhances the grammatical features in the input, and on the other hand, provides L2 learners with opportunities to focus on meaning. Scholars in second language acquisition have agreed that L2 learners must be exposed to input and that input must be comprehensible and meaning-bearing in order to facilitate language development. Language that learners hear and see in communicative contexts forms the data on which the internal mechanisms operate. The only effective way to facilitate language development (implicit knowledge) is the provision of good quality input.

This view about language and language development (too abstract and complex to teach and learn explicitly) has clearly profound consequences for how we implement instruction in the language classroom. Explicit rules and paradigm lists can't become the abstract and complex language system because the two things are completely different. As previously stated, this implication stems from the fact that there is no internal mechanism that can convert explicit textbook rules into our implicit mental representation system. Most textbooks and many teachers continue to treat language like any other subject matter. However, what winds up in the human mind has no resemblance to anything on textbook pages or what teachers say.

The main question is: How do we then provide effective instruction?

1.5 What Are the Main Takeaways?

Let's briefly review some basic facts about language, language acquisition, and language instruction presented in this introduction. These facts will be key in our discussion on the role and effects of focus on form.

- Language is abstract and complex and should not be taught and learned explicitly. There are no known and proved mechanisms that turn explicit 'rules' into the abstract and complex mental representation we call 'language'.
- There is a qualitative difference between explicit and implicit knowledge of language.
- Acquisition is stage-like and ordered. In the acquisition of any structure there are stages that all learners go through regardless of their L1. There is no evidence that stages can be skipped or orders can be altered. Language instruction might therefore have a constrained and limited role.
- Instruction might help L2 learners to develop a good level of attainment particularly if opportunities to natural exposure are given.
- Instruction has a facilitative role when it is used for linguistic features, which are not too distant from the learner's current level of language development. It might have a facilitative role in helping L2 learners to pay selective attention to form and form–meaning connections in the input.

- Although, the route of acquisition cannot be altered, instruction might in certain conditions speed up the rate of acquisition and develop greater language proficiency. What are the conditions that might facilitate the speed in which languages are learned? A first condition is that L2 learners must be exposed to sufficient input. A second condition is that L2 learners must be developmentally ready for instruction to be effective. A third condition is that instruction must take into consideration how L2 learners process input.
- For the research on the effects of instruction to advance, it needs to consider ways in which to assess implicit knowledge along with a consideration of what implicit knowledge actually is.

2 What Are the Key Concepts?

2.1 What Is the Nature of Focus on Form?

Despite the current debate about the role of explicit instruction, scholars (VanPatten, 2016) concur that implicit knowledge is acquired unconsciously. Therefore, for instruction to have a beneficial role, it must consider how people acquire languages and process information in the mind/brain. This means for instance, that instruction should consider the use of pedagogical interventions that create conditions where L2 learners are exposed to the language (forms) while focusing on meaning. It must also consider the key role that input plays in the acquisition of a language. Within this context, focus on form is a type of instruction that draws L2 learners' attention to linguistic elements of the target language while the main focus is on meaning or communication.

Long (1991) makes a clear distinction between two types of instructional pedagogical intervention: 'focus on form' and 'focus on forms'. *Focus on forms* refers to a type of instructional intervention that isolates specific linguistic forms, and teaches them one at the time. In the case of traditional instruction, for example, the instruction is often characterized by paradigmatic explanations of specific linguistic forms or structures, followed by pattern practice and substitution/transformation drills practice. The term *focus on form* is instead characterized by pedagogical interventions which essentially provide L2 learners with a combination of focus on form and focus on meaning. Long (1991) describes focus on form as a language teaching approach which should aim at drawing L2 learner's attention to a particular form incidentally during exposure to language. Long and Robinson (1998: 23) further defined focus on form 'as an occasional shift of attention to linguistic code features – by the teacher and/or one or more students – triggered by perceived problems with comprehension or production'. More recently, Long

(2015: 317) has described focus on form as a pedagogical procedure that 'involves reactive use of a wide variety of pedagogic procedures to draw learners' attention to linguistic problems in context, as they arise during communication'. As explained by Ellis (2016), focus on form has become a set of pedagogical interventions designed to draw L2 learners' attention to a linguistic form in a communicative context. The focus on form can be either pre-planned focusing on a particular form or it can be incidental as L2 learners engage in meaning-based activities. During a focus-on-form intervention the linguistic elements are dealt with either intensively (systematically) or extensively (incidentally), but the primary focus always lies on communication.

Doughty and Williams (1998) and subsequently Ranta and Lyster (2017: 43) have described two types of focus on form: proactive or reactive. Proactive would involve planned instruction (e.g. textual enhancement, processing instruction) designed to enable L2 learners to notice and eventually use the specific target feature. Reactive occurs in response to L2 learners' production and interaction with another interlocutor and includes corrective feedback as well as other attempts to draw learners' attention to the target language.

2.2 What Are the Main Types of Focus on Form?

2.2.1 Input Enhancement

Input enhancement as a type of focus on form was first introduced by Sharwood Smith (1993). It is a pedagogical intervention that aims at helping L2 learners to notice specific forms in the input. In this context, Leow (2001) defines enhanced input as input that has been altered typologically to enhance the saliency of target forms. Input enhancement is an input-based focus on form that exposes L2 learners to comprehensible input and at the same time draws their attention to a specific linguistic property of the target language. Input enhancement varies in terms of explicitness and elaboration. One kind of input-enhancement focus-on-form type consists of modifying a text so that a particular target item appears over and over again. In this way, the text will contain many exemplars of the same feature (i.e. input flood). A different type would consist of underlining, embolding or capitalizing a specific grammatical item (providing typographical cues) in a text (textual enhancement).

Textual enhancement is specifically used to make particular features of written input more salient with the scope to help learners notice these forms and eventually make appropriate form–meaning connections (Benati, 2013). The main characteristic of textual enhancement is to highlight the form in the text (e.g. embolding, underlining) while keeping the learner's attention on

Lisa **goes** to the cinema every weekend. She **likes** Italian films. Sometimes she **plays** tennis golf with me or **goes** to the gym. During the week, she **works** at the University and at the weekend she **drives** to the countryside.

[Text continues]

Follow-up: What kind of things do you like to do at the weekend?

What type of things do you have to do?

Figure 1 Textual enhancement activity (sample)

Last week, Richard worked all day at the University. He jumped out of bed at 8 am. He poured himself three strong cups of coffee to wake up fully. He watched TV and slowly felt more awake. He wanted to go back to sleep again, but he remembered that he had work on Saturdays. He worked part-time at Starbucks café and the Manager was very strict. He walked quickly to the bus stop, but unfortunately there was a lot of traffic and so he waited for over an hour. He eventually arrived late and his manager was extremely angry. He shouted at him and said he was a useless employee. Things got worse when Richard spilled a customer's coffee all over floor and his boss got really angry and informed him that he was sacked. Finally, Richard returned home feeling miserable and exhausted. What a horrible Saturday. At least he could sleep in on Sunday!

[Text continues]

Follow-up: After you hear the text, in pairs, give as many details as you can remember about Richard's horrible day. The group with the most details wins. You have three minutes.

Figure 2 Input Flood activity (sample)

meaning. No metalinguistic explanation is provided during input enhancement (see Figure 1).

Input flood is a type of input enhancement where the input L2 learners receive is saturated with the form that L2 learners should notice. The main characteristic of input flood is that the input L2 learners receive must be modified so that it contains many instances of the same form. The main purpose of this type of focus on form is to help L2 learners notice the form embedded in the input (see Figure 2).

Another type of input enhancement is aural enhancement. This implicit type of focus on form involves the manipulation of listening materials with the aim of making specific linguistic forms more salient in the input. It can include increased volume, slower pace, or short pauses added before and/or after the target items.

2.2.2 Processing Instruction

Processing instruction is a type of focus on form used primarily to facilitate, at input-level, the connection of a linguistic feature to its meaning. Form–meaning connections are the relationships learners make between referential meaning and the way it is encoded linguistically. For example, when learners hear the sentence, *I played tennis in the park* and understand that *played* means the action is in the past, a form–meaning connection is made. This pedagogical intervention is predicated on VanPatten's (1996, 2015a) input processing theory which identifies a number of processing strategies L2 learners use when processing language input.

The first characteristic of processing instruction is to help L2 learners process input more accurately and appropriately. In processing instruction, L2 learners are required to simultaneously focus on form to get meaning so that they improve their ability to process the right information and make the right form–meaning connections during comprehension.

This is a different function from simply noticing a form in the input, as noticing simply means to be consciously aware that the form is there. For example, L2 learners might hear the word *played* and notice that it is different from either *plays* or *playing*. However, they might not immediately connect the ending (e.g. verbal inflection *-ed*) with the concept that the action has already taken place (past event). Processing instruction is fundamentally different from other input-based focus-on-form pedagogical interventions such as input enhancement. This is because enhancing a feature in the input might help L2 learners to notice that feature, but it does not necessarily mean that L2 learners make appropriate form–meaning connections. Processing instruction facilitates both form–meaning connections and accurate processing of sentence structure.

A second characteristic of processing instruction is that it measures the ability of L2 learners to interpret linguistic features contained in the language input. In processing instruction research, rules are not tested (e.g. grammaticality judgement tasks, fill-in-the-gap tasks, etc.), but the ability to process and interpret linguistic features in the input is. A third characteristic is that processing instruction alters the way in which the input is processed by L2 learners, which in turn might have an effect on their language development system. Processing instruction is not intended to assist in skill development, but it might help L2 learners access the right information (form or structure) in order to express meaning.

Processing instruction uses a particular type of input (structured input practice) to push learners away from non-optimal processing strategies so that they are more likely to make correct form–meaning connections or parse sentences (compute basic structure in real time) appropriately during comprehension. It is mainly concerned with the processing of morpho-phonological units in input strings and the development of underlying linguistic representation (Benati, 2019).

Processing instruction consists of two main components:

L2 learners are given explicit information about a linguistic form and the particular processing strategy that may negatively affect their picking up of the form or structure during language processing;

L2 learners are pushed to process (not produce) the form or structure during structured input activities.

Specific guidelines have been established (Lee and VanPatten, 2003) to develop structured input activities (see Figure 3).

- Present one thing at a time.
- Keep meaning in focus.
- Move from sentences to connected discourse.
- Use both oral and written input.
- Have the learners do something with the input.
- Keep the learner's processing strategies in mind.

2.2.3 Corrective Feedback

Corrective feedback is a type of focus on form to which L2 learners' attention can be drawn during an interaction. Lyster and Ranta (1997) originally identified six main types of corrective feedback, and subsequently, Ranta and Lyster (2007) have suggested that each of these six feedback types could be classified

---

Things people did now and last summer
Listen to the following statements and decide whether each statement refers to an activity that takes place now or took place last summer in London.

	NOW	LAST SUMMER
1	☐	☐
2	☐	☐

[the activity continues in similar fashion]
Sentences heard by learners:
1. People visited Buckingham Palace.
2. People protest in London about COVID-19.

Figure 3 Structured input activity (sample)

as either a type of 'reformulation' or a 'prompt'. Reformulations include recasts and explicit correction, whereas prompts are signals that push learners to self-repair without supplying the correct form: elicitations, clarification requests, repetitions of learner error, and metalinguistic explanations and non-verbal feedback. A typical interactional feedback exchange is the following:

> Teacher/NS: Where did you go last summer?
> Student/NNS: I was in vacation in Italy
> Teacher/NS: Oh, where were you on vacation in Italy?
> Student/NNS: I was on vacation in Tuscany

Recast can be defined as teacher's reformulation of all or part of a student's utterance, minus the error. Two main classification of recasts (Nassaji and Fotos, 2011) have been proposed: (a) simple recast deals with minimal changes to the language learner's utterance; (b) complex recast is concerned with providing the language learner with substantial additions. Recast is used by language instructors to make sure that the speaker becomes aware that something is wrong in their speech production. The native speaker (language instructor) provides recast by reformulating the learner's incorrect form into a correct form. The successful correction made by the non-native speaker (language learner) is called uptake. The native speaker continues the interaction in the attempt not to break the flow of communication. The degree of explicitness in using this technique varies also depending on the use of intonational signals. Below is one example of how recast can be used (Lightbown and Spada, 1993: 76):

> NNS: It bugs me when a bee sting me.
> NS: Oh, when a bee stings me.
> NNS: Stings me.
> NS: Do you get stung often?

In this example, the non-native speaker produces a sentence which contains an error. The native speaker (language tutor) provides a recast by reformulating the learner's incorrect form into a correct form. The successful correction made by the non-native speakers is called uptake.

Explicit correction is characterized by an overt and clear indication of the existence of an error and the provision of the target-like reformulation, and it can take two forms: explicit correction and metalinguistic feedback. In explicit correction, the teacher provides both positive and negative evidence by clearly saying that what the L2 learner has produced is erroneous (e.g. You don't say *goed* .... you say *went* .... etc.)

Elicitation is a correction technique that prompts the L2 learner to self-correct and may be accomplished in one of three ways during face-to-face interaction, each of which vary in their degree of implicitness or explicitness. One of these strategies is the request for reformulations of an ill-formed utterance. The second one is through the use of open questions. The last strategy which is the least communicatively intrusive and hence the most implicit is the use of strategic pauses to allow a learner to complete an utterance. With direct elicitation, the NS attempts to elicit relevant information from the non-native speaker. There is no correction but an opportunity for self-repair/correction.

Clarification requests, unlike explicit error correction and recast, can be more consistently relied upon to generate modified output from learners since the request might not supply the learners with any information concerning the type or location of the error. Clarification requests occur when there is a breakdown of communication between two speakers. One speaker asks the other speaker to clarify his/her utterance. It does not provide the speaker with the correct form, however it gives the other speaker the opportunity for self-repair. Phrases such as 'sorry?' or 'what did you say? or 'say it again, please', provide the learner with an opportunity to clarify and/or make his/her utterance more accurate.

Here is an example of clarification requests (from VanPatten and Benati, 2010: 11):

> NNS: I can find no [ruddish].
> NS: *I'm sorry. You couldn't find what?*

Another technique to provide corrective feedback is repetition, which is less communicatively intrusive in comparison to explicit error correction or meta-linguistic feedback and hence falls at the implicit extreme on the continuum of corrective feedback. This type of corrective feedback simply consists of the instructor or interlocutor's repetition of the ill-formed part of the learner's utterance, usually with a change in intonation.

In metalinguistic feedback the focus of conversation with the language learner is diverted towards rules or features of the target language. Metalinguistic feedback is divided into three subcategories: metalinguistic comments, metalinguistic information, and metalinguistic questions. The least informative is metalinguistic comments which only indicate the occurrence of an error. Metalinguistic information not only indicates the occurrence or location of the error but also offers some metalanguage that alludes to the nature of the error. Metalinguistic questions point to the nature of the error but attempt to elicit the information from the learner. Metalinguistic feedback provides the non-native speaker with a metalinguistic cue in the input and/or metalinguistic feedback about the correctness of an utterance.

The example here is from Nassaji and Fotos (2011: 77):

> NNS: I see him in the office yesterday.
> NS: You need a past tense. (metalinguistic cue)

Non-verbal feedback is also another form of corrective feedback. Body move-ments and signals such as gestures, facial expressions, rolling your eyes, crossing your arms, and head, hand, and finger movements are all different forms of feedback. Non-verbal feedback is feedback that the teacher provides to students with their actions (e.g. smiling, patting a student's shoulder, etc.).

2.2.4 Consciousness-Raising Tasks

The goal of consciousness-raising tasks is to make learners conscious of the rules that govern the use of particular language forms while providing the opportunity to engage in meaningful interaction (Nassaji and Fotos, 2011). During conscious-ness-raising tasks, L2 learners develop explicit knowledge about how the target language works and are pushed to negotiate meaning. Explicit knowledge should help L2 learners notice that form in subsequent communicative input, while negotiation of meaning (interaction) can expose learners to more comprehensible input. During consciousness-raising tasks, L2 learners are encouraged to discover grammatical rules. They are provided with some data concerning a particular form and then they are asked to arrive (through completion of a series of sub-tasks) at an explicit understanding of some linguistic property of the specific form. The main purpose of this focus-on-form task is to raise consciousness about a particular form so that L2 learners can notice it in communicative input.

The main characteristics of this type of focus on form is that (i) adequate data are provided to L2 learners to discover the rule and this requires (ii) a minimal production on the part of the learner. A consciousness-raising task (Fotos and Ellis, 1991) provides both a focus on grammatical form and an opportunity for learners to communicate (see Figure 4).

2.2.5 Dictogloss

Dictogloss (Wajnryb, 1990) is a type of collaborative output task which aims at helping L2 learners to use their grammar resources to reconstruct a text and become aware of their own shortcomings and needs. It consists of a listening phase and a reconstruction phase where learners are asked to reconstruct a text rather than write down the exact words that are dictated (see Figure 5, from Benati, 2013: 48). As the text is read at a natural speed, students cannot write down every word but only key words and they have to understand the meaning and use their knowledge of grammar in order to reconstruct it. Dictogloss procedure consists of four stages (see Figure 5): preparation, dictation, recon-struction, and analysis and correction. In dictogloss tasks, the language instructor introduces the main idea of the story and distributes copies of a passage/or reads the passage to the participants (Stage 1).

Step 1

What is the difference in meaning between sentence a and sentence b? What do you think the speaker means?

(a) I was hitting my head against the wall.
(b) I hit a car at 40 miles per hour.

Step 2

Complete the sentences using your own words. What is the difference in meaning between the sentences.

(a) I was working . . . ..
(b) I worked . . . ..
(c) I was talking
(d) I talked . . . ..

Figure 4 Consciousness-raising task

Step 1

Listen to the text and make a note of as many words as you can.

Step 2

Compare your notes with your partner and try to reconstruct the text. Please check carefully for spelling and grammatical accuracy.

Step 3

Compare you version of the text with another pair, and note similarities and differences.

Similar   Different

Figure 5 Dictogloss (sample)

Then, L2 learners are asked to form pairs and work to understand the meaning of the story (Stage 2). The instructor collects the copies from the students, and asks them to reconstruct the passage in pairs as close to the original passage as possible. The instructor stresses the usage of passive voice when appropriate (Stage 3). Finally, the instructor gives back the original passage to the students and asks them to compare their constructed passage to the original passage and make notes on places that are different from the original passage (Stage 4).

2.2.6 Structured Output

Structured output tasks (Lee and VanPatten, 2003) are an effective alternative to mechanical output practice. Structured output activities have two main characteristics: (i) they involve the exchange of previously unknown information; and (ii) they require learners to access a particular form or structure in order to process meaning. Specific guidelines have been established (Lee and VanPatten, 2003) to develop structured output tasks (see Figure 6).

- Present one thing at a time.
- Keep meaning in focus.
- Move from sentences to connected discourse.
- Use both oral and written output.
- Others must respond to the content of the output.
- The learner must have some knowledge of the form or structure.

2.3 How Are the Effects of Focus on Form Measured?

This section will review the main empirical research measuring the effects of focus-on-form types. Overall, experimental studies on the effects of different

Step 1. Indicate if you do each of the following activities *often* or *rarely*.

Activities	Often	Rarely
Play tennis		
Go to the cinema		
Watch Netflix		
Read a newspaper		
Listen to music		

Step 2. Using the information from step 1, create a series of questions to ask your classmate during an interview.
Step 3. Interview your classmate.
Step 4. Prepare a set of statements in which you compare what you do and what your classmate does using the ideas from steps 1, 2, 3. You will present your results to the class and after you have received feedback from other classmates, you will draw some conclusion about students' habits.

Figure 6 Structured output task

types of focus on form have used the same pre- and post-test methodological design (Benati and Schwieter, 2019). In these studies, if L2 learners perform better after instruction, researchers tend to conclude that instruction makes a difference.

In several of the focus-on-form studies conducted to measure instruction, however, there is often a clear bias towards the teaching of explicit knowledge and testing explicit rules through offline tests. There is certainly the need to carry out more research on the effects of focus on form which measure implicit knowledge. This kind of research would also need to adopt psycholinguistics and neurolinguistics research tools which better capture online processing and brain/mind activities to measure implicit knowledge (online tests).

Benati (2020b) has conducted a study to explore the effects of a type of focus on form called structured input on the acquisition of English causative passive forms using online measurements (eye-tracking). The study asked two main questions: (i) What are the effects of structured input and traditional instruction on accuracy when measured by an eye-tracking picture selection task? (ii) Would possible difference in accuracy between structured input and traditional instruction be accompanied by changes in eye-movement patterns? To provide answers to these two questions, one eye-tracking study was carried out. A pre- and post-training design was adopted and subjects were divided into two groups which received two different instructional treatments (structured input vs. traditional instruction). Participants (fifty-two adult learners with Chinese as first language) were assessed through a picture selection eye-tracking task to measure accuracy and eye-movement patterns while they were processing auditory sentences. Results of the eye-tracking task indicated that the structured input group achieved significantly higher accuracy scores compared to the group receiving traditional instruction. The main findings from the study revealed that structured input training causes a change in learners' eye-movement patterns. This study is an example of a focus-on-form study adopting a more appropriate implicit knowledge measurement of the effects of instruction on the acquisition of a formal property of the target language.

2.4 What Are the Key Points to Remember?

- There is a clear distinction between focus on 'form' and focus on 'forms'. Focus on form can be described as any deliberate attempts to draw L2 learners' attention to a particular form in a meaningful context.
- We can distinguish between proactive or reactive type of focus on form.
- Input enhancement is an input-based focus on form that might facilitate L2 learners to notice grammatical forms in the input.

- Processing instruction is an input-based focus on form that might facilitate L2 learners to make form–meaning connections.
- Consciousness-raising tasks might facilitate L2 learners to notice grammatical forms in the input.
- Corrective feedback might facilitate L2 learners to notice forms in the input.
- Collaborative output might facilitate L2 learners to produce output, to promote negotiation of form and at the same time develop learners' linguistic skills.
- Too much of the research is biased towards the testing of explicit knowledge. We need to rethink how we measure the effects of instruction on implicit knowledge, using online testing procedures, for example.

3 What Are the Main Branches of Research?

3.1 What Are the Effects of Input Flood?

Input flood is an implicit and input-based type of focus on form consisting in flooding the input language with a particular linguistic feature with the goal of enhancing the changes for L2 learners to notice and process that feature. The empirical research into the offline and online effects of input flood has mainly been conducted to address the following:

(a) Offline effects of input flood compared to explicit instruction
(b) Offline and online effects of input flood compared to input enhancement types of focus on form

(a) Offline effects of input flood compared to explicit instruction

The offline effects of input flood have been compared in a number of empirical studies. Trahey and White (1993) and Williams and Evans (1998) demonstrated that input flood is an effective pedagogical intervention on the acquisition of adverb placement and participial adjectives and passives in English. However, in the case of Williams and Evans's (1998) study, the effects of input flood were more effective when this treatment was provided in combination with explicit instruction, at least in the case of participial adjective forms. The input flood with or without explicit information was equally effective in the case of the acquisition of passive constructions.

The offline effects of input flood have been measured on the acquisition of Spanish. Hernàndez (2011) investigated the combined effect of explicit instruction and input flood versus input flood alone on learners' use of discourse markers to narrate past events. Even in this case, the main findings showed that both instructional treatments were effective on developing L2 learners' use of discourse markers.

(b) Offline and online effects of input flood compared to input enhancement types of focus on form and jigsaw tasks

Research investigating offline and online effects of input flood versus other types of input enhancement has been conducted across different subjects and languages. Reinders and Ellis (2009) investigated the effects of two types of input flood (enriched group vs. enhanced group). The results of this study showed that both instructional treatments did not help L2 learners noticing the target structure. Similarly, Zyzik and Marqués Pascual (2012) examined the impact of input flood (enhanced vs. input flood only) on L2 learners' ability to recognize and produce differential object marking in Spanish. The main findings from this study indicated that the input flood and the enhanced input flood groups showed modest improvement after the treatment. Szudarski and Carter's study (2016) also indicated limited effects of input flood as they compared two kinds of focus on form on the acquisition of English verb–noun and adjective collocations: input flood only and input flood plus typographical enhancement. Main results from this study indicated that only typographical enhancement resulted in the creation of new knowledge, while the input-flood-only treatment did not.

Choi's (2016) conducted an eye-tracking study measuring enhancement (typographical) vs. unenhanced condition (input flood) on certain collocations. The participants in the two groups did not differ in reading behaviour of known collocations. However, the enhancement group spent significantly more time on unknown sequences than the input flood group. Toomer and Elgort (2019) conducted a study using both online and offline measurements and demonstrated that the enhanced condition was more effective than the reading-only condition (input flood). In particular, the statistical analysis of the results confirmed that the treatment groups developed significant explicit knowledge of the target collocations, with the enhanced condition more effective than the reading-only condition (input flood). No priming effect was shown as a result of typographical enhancement. No implicit knowledge was observed as a result of both typographical enhanced conditions. Evidence of implicit knowledge development was found on the input flood treatment only.

Rahimi et al. (2020) investigated the effects of input flood tasks, unfocused tasks, and jigsaw tasks, on L2 learners' recognition of regular past tense *-ed* in terms of accuracy. The overall results indicated that input flood may promote L2 learners' recognition accuracy of the target form, but this effect may gradually diminish.

A review of the main studies measuring the relative effects of input flood provides the following insights (see a list of representative studies in Table 1):

Table 1 Input flood representative studies

Study	Linguistic Feature/ Language	Subjects/L1	Treatments	Tests	Results
Trahey and White (1993)	English adverb placement	French	Input flood Input flood + EI EI only Control	grammatical judgement contextualized preference oral production	Input flood > Input flood + EI and EI only
Williams and Evans (1998)	English participial adjectives and passives	Various L1s	Input flood Input flood + EI Control	grammatical judgement sentence completion picture-based sentence picture narration	Input flood + EI > Input flood (participial adjectives) Input flood = Input flood + EI (passives)
Szudarski and Carter (2016)	English verb– noun and adjective collocations	Polish	Input flood Input flood + Typographical enhancement Control	Production measures Receptive measures	Input flood + typographical enhancement > Input flood

| Toomer and Elgort (2019) | English low frequency medical collocations | ESL speakers | Input flood Typographical enhancement (bolding) Typographical enhancement (bolding + glossing) | Recall and recognition Lexical-primed | Typographical enhancement (both conditions) > Input flood No priming effects on enhanced condition Input flood > Typographical enhancement (both conditions) |

Note: EI = Explicit information

- Input flood is an effective pedagogical intervention (Trahey and White, 1993) when provided alone or in combination with explicit instruction (Hernàndez, 2011; Williams and Evans 1998).
- Input flood has been compared to other pedagogical treatments such as typographical enhancements (Choi, 2016; Szudarski and Carter, 2016; Toomer and Elgort, 2019) and jigsaw tasks (Rahimi et. al, 2020). The results of these studies are mixed. There is also not enough evidence to show that input flood has a direct effect on developing L2 learners' implicit knowledge.
- Input flood might be an effective focus-on-form type on explicit learning subject to factors such as the length of the treatment and the nature/complexity of the linguistic feature.
- Input flood might increase the chance that L2 learners initially notice a specific target form in the input language they are exposed to, but noticing is not fully guaranteed.

3.2 What Are the Effects of Textual Enhancement?

Textual enhancement is type of focus on form that enhances the saliency of input in written or oral texts with a view to facilitating L2 learners' noticing of targeted forms and thereby enhancing their acquisition. As previously said, textual enhancement makes use of typographical cues (e.g. embolding, italicizing, underlining, colouring, enlarging the font size, etc.) to draw learners' attention to particular forms in a text. From a theoretical point of view, Schmidt's (1995) noticing hypothesis underpins research on textual enhancement. Schmidt (1995: 20) posits that noticing is an essential component of the learning process.

Researchers have used textual enhancements under a variety of conditions and with a variety of intentions. The empirical research into the offline and online effects of textual enhancement has mainly been conducted to address the following:

(a) Offline effects of textual enhancement compared to explicit instruction
(b) Offline effects of textual enhancement compared to other input enhancement types of focus on form
(c) Online effects of textual enhancement compared to other input enhancement types of focus on form

(a) Offline and online effects of textual enhancement compared to explicit instruction

A number of empirical studies investigating the effects of textual enhancement compared to explicit instruction provide mixed results as to the effectiveness of textual enhancement. Doughty (1991) investigated the effectiveness of salient visual clues on the acquisition of English relativization. Overall, the textual enhancement group performed better than the rule-oriented group on both written and aural tests. Subjects receiving the textual enhancement treatment showed better comprehension of content in the text they were exposed to. Such findings allowed the researcher to hypothesize that perceptual salience may have been the main factor in the success of instruction, while the explicit grammar explanation was not. Alanen (1995) carried out a textual enhancement study measuring the acquisition of locative suffixes and consonant changes by native speakers of English reading a semiartificial language resembling Finnish. The overall findings of this study indicated that textual enhancement alone was not a significant factor affecting performance (production). However, on the think-aloud protocol, the results showed that those who read the enhanced texts noticed more of the target forms than those who read unenhanced texts. Online effects of textual enhancement were measured by Cintrón-Valentín and Ellis (2015) in a study investigating the effects of textual enhancement on the acquisition of Latin verb morphology. Eye-tracking data demonstrated that typographical enhancement led to significantly more scrutiny of the verbs compared to a control group, with no differences from the more explicit treatment involving explicit grammar instruction.

(b) Offline effects of textual enhancement compared to other input enhancement types of focus on form

Mixed results were also obtained through empirical studies investigating offline effects of textual enhancement compared to other types of enhancement treatments. Shook (1994) examined the effects of textual enhancement on the acquisition of the Spanish present perfect tense and relative pronouns (*que/ quien*). The overall findings from this classroom study showed that the two groups that read the enhanced texts performed better than the group that read the unenhanced texts on all the assessment tests. Jourdenais et al. (1995) investigated the relative effects of textual enhancement on noticing and producing Spanish preterite and imperfect past tense forms. The analysis of the think-aloud protocols showed no overall significant difference between the enhanced and unenhanced treatments. However, in the written narratives the enhancement group produced significantly more accurate preterite and imperfect forms than the unenhanced group.

White (1998) examined the acquisition of English possessive determiners (his, her) by primary school-level Francophone children. He found that both the textual enhancement and the input flood treatments were effective in improved L2 learners' ability to use the target forms in an oral communication task. Wong

(2002) examined the question whether the level of input (sentence vs. discourse) has an impact on textual enhancement. The target structure was the use of prepositions for geographical locations in French. Overall, the results showed that the two textual enhancement treatments (visual and textual) were better than the unenhanced treatment (input flood) on a paper-and-pencil test. Izumi (2002) exposed two groups to enhanced or unenhanced texts containing relative clauses. Notetaking and think-aloud protocols were used to measure whether or not participants were noticing the target form. Results showed a significant effect for input enhancement in the augmented noticing of the target structure. Simard (2009) investigated the effects of textual enhancement on learners' intake of English third-person singular possessive determiners. Overall, the results showed positive effects for textual enhancement when compared to an unenhanced treatment on an information transfer and a multiple-choice recognition test. LaBrozzi (2014) examined how different types of textual enhancement affect L2 form recognition and reading comprehension on the acquisition of the Spanish preterite tense. Results revealed positive effects for the enhancement treatment (versus the unenhanced treatment) on a translation task, and a multiple-choice test with questions focusing on form or meaning from the text.

A different group of studies have provided less-favourable offline effects for textual enhancement. Overstreet (1998) carried out a study targeting the preterite/imperfect aspectual distinction in Spanish. Enhanced and unenhanced text treatments were compared through a written narration and a true/false comprehension test. He found a significant but negative effect for textual enhancement on comprehension. He hypothesized that the enhancements in the text were too numerous and might have negatively interfered with L2 learners' comprehension of the texts. Leow (1997) measured the effects of textual enhancement and text length on learners' comprehension and intake of Spanish informal imperative verb forms. Enhanced and unenhanced conditions were compared through a multiple-choice comprehension test. The results showed no effects for textual enhancements on comprehension. A second similar study (Leow, 2001) was conducted on the effects of textual enhancement on the acquisition of the Spanish formal imperative. L2 learners were asked to perform a think-aloud as they read the assigned text. The results of this study showed that learners who encountered enhanced forms did not notice more forms than learners who encountered unenhanced forms. Leow et al. (2003) examined the effects of textual enhancement on comprehending and noticing the Spanish present perfect tense and Spanish present subjunctive mood. Subjects were enrolled in a first-year university-level Spanish course. Leow et al. created enhanced and unenhanced versions of two passages, one for each target form. In the enhanced versions, they embolded the tense/mood morpheme, underlined the word containing the morpheme, and increased the character size of the underlined words. Learners performed a think-aloud as they read the passage. Subsequently they performed a multiple-choice comprehension test and a multiple-choice form recognition test. The analysis of the think-aloud protocols showed that textual enhancement had very little effect on the noticing of forms in the input. Lee (2007) conducted an experimental study measuring four different treatments involving textual enhancement and topic familiarity conditions. The responses of the participants were compared with respect to their ability to identify and correct English passive errors and their degree of reading comprehension. The main findings from this study revealed that textual enhancement aided the learning of the target forms while having unfavourable effects on meaning comprehension. Topic familiarity, by contrast, aided learners' comprehension but was ineffective in terms of their learning of the form. In a meta-analytic review of sixteen previous textual enhancement studies, Lee and Huang (2008) explored the overall magnitude of textual enhancement on grammar learning. The authors found a very small effect size for textual enhancement. However, they argued that the mixed results and variations obtained in research investigating the effects of textual enhancement might be the result of a number of factors: different designs adopted, different collection tools and procedures, the difference in the type and number of enhanced cues in the materials, and different objectives pursued in each study. Boers et al. (2017) focused on the potential capability of typographical enhancement to foster the learners' sensitivity to formulaic sequences. Learning was assessed through an episodic memory test. Results highlighted that underlining was effective in improving the learning of formulaic language. However, such benefits did not extend to the unenhanced items, which suggests that typographical enhancement did not boost sensitivity to the formulaic dimension of the text beyond the enhanced items. Meguro (2017) examined the effects of textual enhancement on the acquisition of tag questions in English. Reading comprehension was assessed using a multiple-choice grammar task based on information from the passage. He found limited and mixed effects for textual enhancement on learning tag questions.

(c) Online effects of textual enhancement alone or compared to other input enhancement types of focus on form

The majority of studies measuring online effects of textual enhancement demonstrated a positive effect for this treatment. Simard and Foucambert's (2013) study addressed both online (eye tracking) and offline (verbal reports) measures of noticing. Eye-tracking measures showed increased consciousness in participants when reading enhanced compared to unenhanced input. Issa et al. (2015) compared the effects of typographical enhancement (red colouring) and structured input activities on the reading and learning of Spanish direct object pronouns. Analysis of eye-tracking data on skipping rates showed that both interventions significantly improved the amount of attention paid to the target items as compared with the control group, with no difference between input enhancement and structured input activities. Alsadoon (2015) investigated the impact of textual input enhancement on the noticing and intake of English vowels by Arabic L2 learners of English. An eye-tracker recorded participants' eye fixations during the treatment phase. Overall, main findings indicated that vowel blindness was significantly reduced for the experimental group who received vowel training in the form of textual input enhancement. Indrarathne and Kormos (2016) assigned their subjects to the following type of exposure to form: typographical enhancement (boldface; explicit instructions to pay attention to the enhanced words and metalinguistic explanation; typographical enhancement and explicit instructions; typographical enhancement with no explicit instructions; unenhanced text. Eye tracking showed that enhancement, even without explicit instruction for participants to pay attention to it, resulted in longer fixations on the target items (causative had constructions), that is, it positively affected levels of consciousness. Lee and Révész (2020) assessed the effects of textual enhancement through an eye-tracking study. The target L2 construction was the use of the present perfect versus the past simple in reporting news. A series of mixed-effects models found textual enhancement effective in drawing L2 learners' attention to and facilitating development in the use of the target construction.

Winke (2013) used eye-movement data to measure textual enhancement. This study aimed at assessing whether English passive construction enhancement affects English language learners in terms of learning the form and improving text comprehension. The main findings of this study are different from Lee's (2007). Winke (2013) found that enhancement did not have an effect on learning the target forms. However, it did have a significant impact on the ability of learners to notice the passive forms in the text.

The results of the research on the effects of textual enhancements are quite mixed. A review of the main studies measuring the relative effects of textual enhancement provide the following insights (see Table 2 with representative studies):

• A number of textual enhancement studies measuring L2 development provided evidence for the favourable effects of textual enhancement (e.g. Indrarathne and Kormos, 2016; Izumi, 2002; Jourdandenais et al., 1995; LaBrozzi, 2014;

Table 2 Textual enhancement representative studies

Study	Linguistic Feature/ Language	Subjects/ L1	Treatments	Tests	Results
Shook (1994)	Spanish perfect tense and relative pronouns	English	No enhancement Textual enhancement Textual enhancement + EI	Multiple choice Recognition test Cloze production	Textual Enhancement = Textual Enhancement + EI > No enhancement
Leow (1997)	Spanish informal imperative forms	English	Enhanced Unenhanced	Multiple choice comprehension	No effects for enhanced treatment
White (1998)	English possessive determiners	French	Input flood + textual enhancements Input flood + textual enhancements + extensive reading and listening Input flood only	Oral picture description	All three treatments performed equally
Wong (2002)	Prepositions for geographical locations in French	English	Enhanced (bolding and italics) Unenhanced Enhanced (visually)	Written paper-and-pencil test	Enhanced treatments better than unenhanced treatment

Table 2 (cont.)

Study	Linguistic Feature/ Language	Subjects/ L1	Treatments	Tests	Results
Issa et al (2015)	Spanish direct object pronouns	English	Input enhancement Structured input Control	Eye-tracking task	Input enhancement = Structured input > Control

Lee, 2007; Lee and Révész, 2020; Shook, 1994; Simard, 2009; White, 1998; Wong, 2002).
- Others studies found no significant or limited effects for textual enhancement (e.g. Alanen, 1995; Boers et al., 2017; Leow, 1997, 2001, 2003; Meguro, 2017; Overstreet, 1998; Winke, 2013).
- The meta-analysis conducted by Lee and Huang (2008) showed very little effect of textual enhancement. However, they found that learners who were exposed to enhancement-embedded texts showed slight improvement from before to after the treatment.
- Empirical findings show more agreement when it comes to the effects of textual enhancement on attention allocation. Three main tools have been employed in order to investigate how typographical enhancement affects attention: notetaking (Izumi, 2002), think-aloud protocols (Leow et al., 2003) and eye tracking (Cintron-Valentin and Ellis, 2015; Indrarathne and Kormos 2016; Issa et al., 2015; Lee and Révész, 2020; Winke 2013). The majority of these online and offline studies confirmed that typographical enhancement increased the amount of attention paid to the target items.
- Overall, the existing empirical research measuring the effects of textual enhancement has shown small-sized positive effects. However, different researchers have come to different conclusions on the efficacy of input enhancement. A number of factors might constrain the effects of input enhancement on the acquisition of grammar: proficiency level, the developmental stage and the degree of readiness of the learner, the type of linguistic feature chosen, and the intensity of the treatment.

It is important for findings on input enhancement and its role in awareness and attention to be confirmed in online studies employing a more fine-grained measure (i.e. eye tracking). Even if product-level tests fail to highlight new knowledge, eye movements measured at the process level in different studies show the effectiveness of textual enhancement in terms of amount of attention paid to target items.

3.3 What Are the Effects of Processing Instruction?

Offline effects of processing instruction have been widely investigated (Benati, 2019; Benati and Lee, 2015; Benati and Schwieter, 2017; Lee, 2015) using a variety of languages (e.g. Arabic, French, German, Greek, Italian, Japanese, Russian, Spanish), linguistic features (e.g. word order, clitic pronouns, passive and causative constructions, tense markers, aspectual markers, mood with expression of doubt), populations (groups and individuals from eight different L1s) and contexts. To measure the offline effects of processing instruction and compare it to other pedagogical interventions, two methodological designs have been used: pre-test and post-test (immediate and delayed) experimental design; and the so-called trials-to-criterion design. The latter is a methodological design used to examine the possible effects of the treatment itself (number of trials needed for learners to correctly process sentences) and L2 learners' reaction times in sentence responses.

The empirical research into the offline effects of processing instruction has mainly been conducted to address the following:

(a) Offline effects of processing instruction compared to other pedagogical interventions
(b) Offline effects of processing instruction at discourse level
(c) Offline durative effects of processing instruction
(d) Offline secondary effects of processing instruction
(e) Offline effects of structured input activities
(f) Online effects of structured input and processing instruction

(a) Offline effects of processing instruction compared to other pedagogical interventions

Processing instruction is an effective type of focus on form which has consistently demonstrated significant improvement in L2 learner's performance on both interpretation and production sentence-level tasks. In interpretation tasks, learners are normally required to interpret sentences containing the target feature. In production tasks, L2 learners are asked to put verbs in the correct form by completing a short passage or producing a series of sentences containing the target form. The offline effects of processing instruction, investigated in a number of empirical studies, have shown that it is a better instructional intervention than traditional instruction (paradigmatic explanations of rules followed by drill and mechanical practice) for improving learners' rate of processing and for increasing their accuracy in production (VanPatten and Cadierno, 1993; VanPatten and Wong, 2004). The effects of processing instruction have also been compared to other instructional interventions, such as meaning-based output instruction (Farley, 2004; Benati, 2005), and input-based interventions (Lee and Benati, 2007a). These comparative studies demonstrate that processing instruction is better than other pedagogical interventions for circumventing learners' processing problems when measured by offline tasks. This branch of empirical research has also demonstrated that processing instruction can help L2 learners of any target language (Romance and non-Romance languages) develop an appropriate target-language-specific processing strategy to address a target-language-specific processing problem.

Processing instruction offline research has examined native speakers (NSs) of English learning Romance languages (French, Italian, Spanish) and non-Romance languages such as English, German, Japanese and Russian. Other studies (Benati and Lee, 2015) have examined NSs of Chinese, Greek, Italian, Korean, and Turkish, learning English as an L2. Processing instruction seems also to be effective for instilling target-language-specific processing strategies no matter the native language of the learners.

(b) Offline effects of processing instruction at discourse level

Positive results of processing instruction have been observed on discourse-level tasks (interpretation and production). Benati and Lee (2010) found positive effects of processing instruction using discourse-level interpretation tasks on a variety of languages and linguistic forms (e.g. English past tense, Japanese passive constructions). Benati and Batziou (2017, 2019) have demonstrated that processing instruction has positive effects on discourse-level production tasks (oral and written video-based retellings, and oral and written structured interview).

(c) Offline durative effects of processing instruction

The original processing instruction study by VanPatten and Cadierno (1993) demonstrated that the effects of processing instruction were retained one month after instruction. Many subsequent studies have included delayed post-testing that shows learners retain the benefits of processing instruction, with the post-testing taking place one week after instruction (Lee and Benati 2007b), after two weeks (Benati 2013b), after three weeks (Benati, 2005), after six weeks (VanPatten, Farmer and Clardy, 2009), after six months (Benati and Batziou, 2019), and after eight months (VanPatten and Fernández, 2004). The effects of processing instruction were measured using a variety of offline tasks including aural interpretation, oral or written production, form selection, and guided composition.

(d) Offline secondary effects of processing instruction

Benati and Lee (2008) examined the transfer-of-training effects of processing instruction. 'Transfer-of-training effects' was defined as the effects of the processing instruction treatment used to help learners process a particular form affected by a specific processing principle that is transferred to another linguistic form affected by the same processing principle. For instance, they provided processing instruction training to L2 learners on Italian noun-adjective gender agreement and found that it transferred to the future tense. Benati and Lee (2008) found that training on the English past tense marker -*ed* is transferred to the third person singular present tense marker -*s*. They also trained L2 learners to process imperfective verb morphology in French and found that it transferred to subjunctive forms. Processing instruction therefore seems to have primary and secondary effects on similar morphological or syntactic constructions.

(e) Offline effects of structured input activities

One branch of research within the processing instruction research agenda has investigated which factor is the most effective component in the processing instruction pedagogical intervention. Is it the explicit information component or the structured input practice? Or perhaps both components together are the causative factors in making this pedagogical intervention effective? The original study which attempted to address these questions was conducted by Van Patten and Oikkenon (1996). Fifty-nine subjects participated in this classroom experiment. The students were studying Spanish in secondary school and were in their second year. The item investigated was the object pronouns in Spanish and the processing principle under investigation was the First Noun Principle. Three groups were compared: one received only explicit instruction, the other the structured input practice, and the third both components (full processing instruction). The results of this study demonstrated that processing instruction and the structured input group made similar gains whereas the explicit information only group did not. The statistical analyses revealed that the gains made (on both the interpretation and production tasks) by both the processing instruction and the structured input only group were greater than the group receiving only explicit instruction on the targeted form. The main outcome of this study was that structured input practice was the causative variable for the positive results obtained by learners on the two tasks. The structured input practice group performed as well as the processing instruction group in the interpretation and the production tests. These findings strongly suggest that it is the structured input tasks themselves that are responsible for improvement in learners. Benati (2004a, 2004b), and Lee and Benati (2007b) replicated the original experimental conducted by VanPatten and Oikkenon (1996) and obtained similar results. The effectiveness of structured input practice was generalized to different learner backgrounds and L1s, different forms/structures (verbal and nominal morphology), different processing strategies (primacy of meaning principle and its corollaries) and languages (Romance languages and Japanese), and confirmed the findings obtained that it is the structured input component that is responsible for L2 learners improved performance (see Lee and Benati, 2009, for a full review of research measuring the effects of structured input).

Overall, the main findings from research measuring offline effects of processing instruction on the interpretation and processing of target forms or structures has revealed the following:

- It is an effective type of focus on form. Learners with different first languages (L1s) and backgrounds make consistent gains in interpretation and production tests at sentence and discourse-level;
- The effects of processing instruction are consistent, durative, and measurable for different languages and processing problems;
- L2 learners who receive training in one type of processing strategy for one specific form transfer the use of that strategy to other forms without further instruction.

Despite the large database, investigation within the processing instruction research framework has primarily made use of listening and reading measures (so-called off-line measures) to discern how L2 learners comprehend and process sentences. Online methods such as eye tracking and self-paced reading have now been incorporated into processing instruction research to measure language processing more directly and efficiently. The primary aim of processing instruction is to steer L2 learners away from input processing strategies that prevent them from (correctly) linking form and meaning during real-time comprehension. Dozens of studies utilizing pre-/post-test designs conducted over almost thirty years show that L2 learners who receive processing instruction (or structured input alone) make significant gains in comprehension from pre- to post-test, as measured by offline, sentence-level and discourse-level interpretation tasks. However, until very recently, processing instruction research has not included online measures of processing in pre-test and post-test assessments, which are needed to show that L2 learners adopt new strategies for processing input in real time. The use of online methods to measure the effects of processing instruction might offer us the possibility of more fine-grained information and analysis about moment-by-moment sentence comprehension and even a way to better measure implicit knowledge.

(f) Online effects of structured input and processing instruction

Self-paced reading studies

Henry (2015) compared processing instruction with traditional instruction on the acquisition of German accusative case markers. Henry tested German object-first sentences, which L2 learners tend to misinterpret as subject-first sentences due to reliance on the FNP. He administered a processing instruction (and a processing instruction treatment + prosody) treatment that pushed learners to rely on case-marked determiners instead of word order for information about grammatical roles. He also included a third treatment (traditional instruction) that reflected more traditional grammar instruction. Prior to and after instruction, participants completed a self-paced reading task in which they read SVO and OVS sentences phrase by phrase. Compared to learners who received traditional instruction, learners who received processing instruction (and processing instruction + prosody) had longer reading times on the critical NPs after instruction, which suggests that PI pushed learners to direct overt attention to NPs (presumably to attend to the case-marked determiners). However, reading times on case-marked NPs did not differ between SVO and OVS sentences, as was expected if learners were using case markings to override the FNP online. The main results of this study showed that the processing group outperformed the traditional instruction group on an offline comprehension task, but there were no differences between the two groups on the self-paced reading measure.

Chiucchiu and Benati (2020) investigated the effects of structured input and textual enhancement on the acquisition of the Italian subjunctive of doubt using a self-paced reading test. The main questions of this study are: Would L2 learners exposed to structured input and textual enhancement demonstrate sensitivity to violations of the Italian subjunctive of doubt as measured by a self-paced reading test? Would L2 learners exposed to structured input and textual enhancement demonstrate the ability to comprehend sentences containing subjunctive of doubt? Chinese learners of Italian were assigned to two instructional groups: structured input or textual enhancement. The main results from the self-paced reading task indicated that only the structured input group showed higher sensitivity to violations and this group improved from pre-test to post-test in the ability to comprehend sentences containing the target feature under investigation.

Eye-tracking studies

More recently, eye tracking has been used in processing instruction research to measure the location and duration of eye gazes while speech unfolds. Wong and Ito (2018) conducted two experiments that compared the effects of processing instruction and traditional instruction on L2 French learners' processing of the French causative construction, in which the agent of a caused action appears post-verbally (literal translation to English: *Pierre makes to make coffee to Marie*) instead of pre-verbally as in English (*Pierre makes Marie make coffee*). Prior to and after training with processing instruction or traditional instruction, participants completed a visual world eye-tracking task in which they heard French causative and non-causative (the equivalent of *Pierre makes coffee for Marie*) sentences and had to select via mouse click which of two pictures (e.g. one of Pierre making coffee for Marie or one of Marie making coffee for Pierre) best matched the spoken sentence. In Experiment 1, the instructional treatments lacked explicit information, whereas in Experiment 2 they included it. Prior to instruction in both experiments, both groups gazed at the incorrect picture throughout causative sentences. After instruction, the processing instruction group looked significantly more often to the correct picture towards the end of causative sentences, with and without explicit information, whereas the traditional instruction group only did so when provided explicit information. Although the authors expected the shift in looks to the correct picture to begin sooner (i.e. immediately after hearing the second verb in the conjoined VP), the fact that a difference in looks emerged prior to sentence offset strongly suggests that processing instruction affects the strategies that learners use to process input in real time. This is significant considering that the processing instruction group only saw twenty-four causative sentences during training.

In a pair of follow-up experiments, Ito and Wong (2019) tested whether consistency in input modality (i.e. auditory processing instruction training prior to the visual world task) might lead to an earlier shift in looks to the correct picture. They also manipulated voice familiarity (same vs. different) across training and online task. Surprisingly, the auditory processing instruction training led to a longer delay in the use of online cues to sentence structure during spoken language comprehension in that looks to the correct picture did not increase until after sentence offset, regardless of voice familiarity.

Lee and Doherty (2018) compared native and non-native processing of active and passive sentences in Spanish. Accuracy and response time were measured in a paired picture-matching task. After receiving processing instruction, the non-native speakers showed no significant difference from the native speakers in accuracy and response time. The behaviour of the non-native participants became more native-like after exposure to processing instruction.

Benati (2020) explored the effects of structured input and traditional instruction on the acquisition of English causative passive forms using online measurements (eye tracking). The main questions of this study are: (i) What are the effects of structured input and traditional instruction on accuracy when measured by an eye-tracking picture selection task?; (ii) Would possible difference in accuracy between structured input and traditional instruction be accompanied by changes in eye-movement patterns? A pre- and post-training design was used for this experiment. Participants were assessed through a picture selection eye-tracking task to measure accuracy and eye-movement patterns while they were processing auditory sentences. Results of the eye-tracking task indicated that the structured input group achieved significantly higher accuracy scores compared to the group receiving traditional instruction. The main findings from the present study reveal that structured input training causes a change in learners' eye-movement patterns.

The initial findings of this new line of research (measuring online effects of processing instruction) does provide some initial evidence (see Table 3 for list of representative studies):

· Processing instruction and/or structured input alters the strategies that L2 learners use to process input in real time. This new line of enquiry (Benati, 2019, forthcoming) is currently limited to five empirical studies, one principle (the First Noun Principle), a few target structures (object first sentences, passive and causative constructions), four languages (German, Spanish, English, and French), and two online methods (self-paced tests and eye-tracking). This line of research (online testing) in processing instruction is very much in its infancy. It needs to be expanded to include a wider variety of input processing principles, L2s, target forms and structures, and different online methods to collect data.

3.4 What Are the Effects of Corrective and Interactional Feedback?

Corrective feedback (constitutes a reactive type of focus on form that occurs in both the negotiation of meaning and of form) involves (see the following example with key components) a number of different strategies that can be classified in terms of whether they are implicit/explicit and input-providing /output-prompting strategies. Research on corrective feedback is presented making a distinction between reformulations and prompts.

(a) Teacher: What did you do on the weekend?
(b) Student: We went to a fieldtrip. Trigger
(c) Teacher: Oh, you went on a fieldtrip. Feedback
(d) Student: Yeah, went on a fieldtrip. Uptake

A substantial body of research has investigated the role corrective feedback. The empirical research into the offline and online effects of corrective feedback has mainly been conducted to address the following:

(a) Studies supporting a positive role for recasts
(b) Studies showing a limited role for recasts
(c) Studies showing positive effects of prompts as a type of corrective feedback.

Table 3 Processing instruction representative studies

Study	Linguistic Feature/ Language	Subjects/ L1	Treatments	Tests	Results
VanPatten and Cadierno (1993)	Spanish direct object pronouns	English	Processing instruction Traditional instruction Control	Interpretation Production (sentence-level)	PI > TI and C (interpretation) PI = TI > C (production)
VanPatten and Oikkenon (1996)	Spanish direct object pronouns	English	Processing instruction Structured input Explicit information	Interpretation Production (sentence-level)	PI = SI > EI (interpretation) PI = SI > EI (production)
Benati and Batziou (2019)	English causative forms	Greek	Structured input Structured output Combination (SI +SO)	Interpretation Production (sentence-level) Interpretation (discourse-level)	• PI = SI + SO > SO • (interpretation) • PI = SI + SO > SO • (production) • PI = SI + SO > SO • (interpretation discourse)
VanPatten and Fernández (2004)	Spanish direct object pronouns	English	Processing instruction Traditional instruction	Interpretation Production (sentence-level)	PI > TI (interpretation) PI = TI (production) Effects for PI maintained in delayed post-tests up to six months

Table 3 (cont.)

Study	Linguistic Feature/ Language	Subjects/ L1	Treatments	Tests	Results
Benati and Lee (2008)	Italian noun-adjective agreement and future tense	English	Processing instruction Traditional instruction Control	Interpretation Production (sentence-level)	Primary effects PI > TI and C (interpretation) PI = TI > C (production) Secondary effects PI > TI and C
Wong and Ito (2018)	French causative constructions	English	Structured input Traditional instruction	Eye tracking picture selection task	SI > TI

Note: PI = Processing instruction – TI = Traditional instruction – C = Control – SI = Structured input – SO = Structured output – EI = Explicit information

3.4.1 Reformulations

(a) Studies supporting a positive role for recasts

Doughty and Varela (1998) compared the performance of two groups of young learners in a content-based classroom. The main results from this study showed that L2 learners in the corrective recasting group – which included a repetition of the error followed by recasts – outperformed the other group which received no feedback. Han (2002) examined the contribution of corrective feedback in the form of recasts to the acquisition of tense consistency. He found out that due to their heightened awareness, L2 learners in the recast group were more successful in both oral and written tests in comparison to the group receiving no corrective feedback. Loewen and Philp (2006) investigated the role of recasts and showed it as effective as other forms of feedback (metalinguistic feedback and elicitations). Several characteristics of recasts (i.e. intonation, interrogative, stress emphasis) were identified as more likely to predict successful learners' uptake. Egi (2007) found that when recasts were long and substantially different from their problematic utterances, L2 learners tended to interpret them as responses to content. Therefore, Egi concluded that the length of recast and number of changes might partially determine the explicitness of recasts and thus affected L2 learners' interpretation. Go and Mackey (2013) reviewed empirical studies on the effectiveness of recasts and argued against those that supported the relative ineffectiveness of recasts. They supported the view that recasts generate a high rate of uptake. Rassaei (2020) provided evidence for the effectiveness of recasts when combined with textual enhancement on L2 development, as measured by a picture-story task and a story-writing task.

(b) Studies showing a limited role for recasts

Lyster and Ranta (1997) found out that only a small percentage of recast lead to learner's uptake. Corrective feedback can only lead to repair and uptake when there is negotiation of form. Lyster (1998) discovered that the corrective force entailed in recasts might easily go unnoticed by learners due to its implicit nature. Panova and Lyster (2002) also confirmed that the rate of learners' uptake following recast is very low, lower than in the case of elicitations techniques. Nabei and Swain (2002) found that the majority of recasts did not provide an opportunity for repair. Sheen's (2007) study also indicated that the rate of learner uptake following recast was the lowest of all feedback types. Carpenter, Jeon, MacGregor, and Mackey (2006) showed that L2 learners were significantly less successful at distinguishing recasts from repetitions.

Mackey and Philp (1998) discovered that learners who were developmentally ready benefited more from interaction that contained recasts than those who received interaction that did not contain recasts. Lyster (2004) investigated the differential effects of recasts and prompts. The results indicated that the recast group was inferior to the prompt group. This limited effectiveness of recasts and the superiority of prompts was further reported by Ammar and Spada (2006) and Lyster and Izquierdo (2009). One of the major explanations they proposed for the superiority of prompt over recast was its explicitness. That is, prompt was more explicit than recast and thus highlighted the teacher's corrective objective, which was far less explicit and quite ambiguous in recast. Ellis, Loewen, and Erlam (2006) compared the effectiveness of implicit and explicit corrective feedback on low-intermediate learners' performance. To measure the implicit knowledge, an oral imitation test was employed while in order to tap into the learners' explicit knowledge, a grammaticality judgement test in addition to a metalinguistic knowledge test were used. The statistical analysis indicated the superiority of explicit feedback over the implicit type for both delayed imitation and grammaticality judgement test.

As indicated in a number of empirical studies, there is a tendency for classroom learners receiving explicit correction to demonstrate greater gains than learners receiving recasts (e.g. Ellis, Loewen and Erlam, 2006; Sheen, 2007; Nassaji, 2017).

Nassaji (2009) investigated the effectiveness of recasts and elicitation in dyadic interaction. The feedback types were further categorized with respect to implicitness and explicitness. The explicit forms of both feedback types resulted in higher rates of correction than their implicit forms. Granena and Yilmaz (2019) investigated the relative effects of implicit (reformulations) and explicit feedback on gender agreement and differential object marking in Spanish, when measured by means of a self-paced reading task. The results showed that neither explicit nor implicit feedback had an effect on L2 learners' grammatical sensitivity to the target structures and, therefore, that feedback was not effective in changing L2 learning outcomes, as measured through an online processing measure.

3.4.2 Prompts

(c) Studies showing positive effects of prompts as a type of corrective feedback.

Results of quasi-experimental research comparing the effects of different types of prompts can be summarized as follows. Lyster and Saito (2010) conducted a meta-analysis of fifteen classroom-based feedback studies. Corrective feedback was effective and had a lasting effect on learning. Prompts, recasts, and explicit correction all had significant effects, with medium effects for recasts and large effects for prompts. Oral corrective feedback was significantly more effective than no corrective feedback (e.g. Doughty and Varela, 1998; Saito and Lyster, 2012). There was a tendency for classroom learners receiving prompts to demonstrate more gains on some measures than L2 learners receiving recasts. For example, in the case of young immersion students, recasts and prompts were equally effective in oral production measures, but, additionally, prompts were more effective in written production measures (Lyster, 2004). Recasts and prompts were equally effective for young ESL learners with high pre-test scores, but prompts were more effective than recasts for L2 learners with low pre-test scores (Ammar and Spada, 2006). Adult EFL learners in China benefitted equally from recasts and prompts in improving accuracy of irregular past tense forms, but prompts were more effective than recasts in improving their accurate use of regular forms (Yang and Lyster, 2010).

Although some mixed results have been found on the role of corrective feedback as a type of focus on form, the initial findings do provide some good insights for language learning (see also list of representative studies in Table 4):

- Corrective feedback might be more effective by using additional intonational prompts, by providing enough exposure to the correct form, and when targeting a single linguistic feature at a time (Go and Mackey, 2013).
- The effectiveness of corrective feedback might also be affected by developmental sequences (Mackey and Philp (1998). Learners learn a form when they are developmentally ready. Therefore, for corrective feedback to be effective, language instructors should match the feedback with L2 learners' developmental stages.
- The effects of corrective feedback may not be immediate but gradual and not all grammar forms respond equally to corrective feedback.
- L2 learners may notice lexical errors more effectively than morphosyntactic errors.
- Corrective feedback with uptake is more effective than feedback with no uptake.
- It may not be possible for researchers to identify the single most effective type of feedback (Ellis, 2012; Lyster, Saito and Sato, 2013). Instead, language instructors may be well advised to orchestrate a range of feedback types. To do so, they need to make choices in accordance with a host of factors including linguistic targets, interactional contexts, students' age and proficiency, and curricular objectives (Lyster et al., 2013). Use of only one type of corrective feedback could never cover all these bases, because, as Ammar and Spada (2006: 556) concluded, 'one size does not fit all'.

Table 4 Corrective feedback representative studies

Study	Linguistic Feature/ Language	Subjects/ L1	Treatments	Tests	Results
Doughty and Varela (1998)	English Past and Conditional	French	Recasts Control (no correct-ive feedback	Oral presentation	Recasts > Control
Ammar and Spada (2006)	English third person possessive determiners	French	Recasts Prompts	Written and Oral tasks	Prompts > Recasts
Lyster and Ranta (1997)	French	English	Explicit correction Recasts Clarification requests Metalinguistic feedback Elicitation Repetition	Speech production measures	Recasts does not lead to repair and uptake Corrective feedback lead to repair and uptake only when there is negotiation of form
Mackey and Philp (1998)	English question formation	Various L1s	Intensive Recasts No Recasts	Information gap tasks	Recasts > No Recasts

3.5 What Are the Effects of Output and Collaborative Focus on Form Tasks?

3.5.1 Consciousness-Raising Tasks

Consciousness-raising tasks are a form of focus on form which requires L2 learners to work collaboratively to complete a grammatical analysis of some kind, either inductively or deductively. However, most consciousness-raising tasks in the existing literature tend to be inductive and text-driven. Such tasks typically consist of a text that students read and discuss for its meaning, before they focus on the target form. Unfortunately, there is no sufficiently large research database measuring the relative effects of this type of focus on form. The empirical research into the relative effects of consciousness raising has provided mixed results and it has mainly been conducted to address offline effects of consciousness-raising tasks.

Fotos and Ellis (1991) conducted the first study measuring the possible effectiveness of consciousness-raising tasks among Japanese learners of English. They compared consciousness-raising tasks with traditional teacher-fronted grammar instruction. Fotos and Ellis (1991) concluded that the consciousness-raising task appeared to have functioned equally well as the grammar lesson in the short term.

Yip (1994) investigated whether consciousness-raising tasks can help ESL learners overcome errors in the usage of ergative verbs. A grammaticality judgement task and an error correction task were used to measure the effectiveness of consciousness-raising tasks. One of the two groups receiving consciousness-raising tasks showed significant improvement in their scores from pre to post-tests.

Fotos (1994) conducted an empirical study on this particular focus on form. Subjects consisted of Japanese learners of English. Two groups were compared: one receiving consciousness-raising tasks and another traditional grammar instruction. Fotos (1994) used game-like tasks with cards that either guided learners towards formulating rules or working with a given rule. The two groups performed equally on the assessment tasks. The consciousness-raising type of focus on form was successful in promoting a significant level of noticing the target structures in the input.

Sugiharto (2006) investigated Indonesian learners' ability in understanding the simple present tense rules. Using a grammatical judgement test, he conducted a 'one shot' study to compare results from pre-and post-test. He found that L2 learners performed well on the post-test. This study indicated that consciousness raising is effective in helping L2 learners develop their explicit knowledge of the target form. Data-driven learning is another type of consciousness-raising task through the use of corpora and concordances. Smart (2014) evaluated the effectiveness of this type of consciousness-raising task using paper-based concordances drawn from a corpus. This type of focus on form consists of four stages: data illustration; interaction with the data; intervention by the teacher who provides hint; learners need to make their own rule. Smart found the concordance-based task to have had a beneficial effect on L2 learning of the passive in English.

The initial findings of research measuring the relative effects of consciousness-raising tasks does provide some initial evidence (see representative studies in Table 5):

- Consciousness raising is at least as effective, and in certain cases better than, traditional instruction and in developing in l2 learners' explicit knowledge about a target form (Fotos and Ellis, 1991).
- Consciousness raising is providing L2 learners a focus on form with good opportunities for interaction and communication in the language classroom (Fotos, 1994).

3.5.2. Dictlogoss

Dictogloss is a type of focus on form in which a meaning-based context is provided for L2 learners to focus their attention on in the use of a particular form while communicating with each other. Unfortunately, there is no enough research measuring the relative effects of this type of collaborative focus on form. The empirical research into the relative effects of dictogloss has mainly been conducted to address the following:

(a) Observing the effects of dictogloss
(b) Comparing the effects of dictogloss with other pedagogical interventions

(a) Observing the effects of dictogloss

Positive effects of dictogloss have been found in a number of empirical studies. Nabei (1996) examined learners' interaction during a dictogloss task. The main findings of this study indicated that it facilitates discussion of both meaning and form among L2 learners. Lim and Jacobs (2001) investigated the performance and behaviour of L2 learners while performing a dictogloss task. The findings of the study provided evidence that peer collaboration during this type of task between participants resulted in a better learning environment. Several empirical studies have shown that dictogloss is a task that promotes attention to form in a meaningful context (Alegría de la Colina and García Mayo, 2007; Basterrechea and García Mayo, 2013; Basterrechea, García Mayo and Leeser, 2014; García Mayo, 2002).

Table 5 Consciousness raising representative studies

Study	Linguistic Feature/ Language	Subjects/ L1	Treatments	Tests	Results
Fotos and Ellis (1991)	English dative alterations	Japanese	Consciousness raising Traditional instruction	Grammatical judgement tasks	Consciousness raising = Traditional instruction
Fotos (1994)	English ondirect object placement adverb placement relative clause	Japanese	Consciousness raising Traditional instruction	Problem-solving tasks	Consciousness raising = Traditional instruction

Kuiken and Vedder (2002) examined the effectiveness of learners' interaction during a dictogloss task on acquiring grammar. The results showed that the interaction between learners during the reconstruction stage did not lead to any improvement in terms of use of particular forms/ structures in the written texts.

(b) Comparing the effects of dictogloss with other pedagogical interventions

Mixed results have been found in studies comparing dictogloss with text reconstruction. Swain and Lapkin (2001) compared the effects of a dictogloss task and a jigsaw task in terms of L2 learners' task performance. The results showed no difference between the two the two tasks in terms of learners' performance. The quality of reconstructed stories and learning outcome were the same. García Mayo (2002) investigated the effects of two focus-on-form tasks: dictogloss and text reconstruction. The findings indicated that dictogloss is more effective than text reconstruction.

Yeo (2002), compared dictogloss with an input enhancement technique. The results of the study indicated that the group in which dictogloss was used by L2 learners outperformed the other group of learners who were exposed to an input enhancement task.

Leeser (2004) studied L2 learners' proficiency level and focus on form through the use of the dictogloss and analysed language-related episodes (LREs). The findings suggested that as the proficiency level of the learners increased, the number of LREs which were produced also increased and these LREs became more grammatical in nature.

Qin (2008) compared dictogloss to processing instruction on the acquisition of English passive voice. Results showed that the processing instruction group performed significantly better than the dictogloss group in comprehension, and as well as the dictogloss group in production on the immediate post-test. One month later, the two groups performed similarly in terms of both comprehension and production on the delayed post-test. VanPatten, Inclezan, Salazar, and Farley (2009) also compared the effects of dictogloss and processing instruction in a partial replication of Qin's study. In their study, they found processing instruction superior overall to dictogloss both in immediate and delayed post-tests.

HoKang (2009) examined the effects of dictogloss on both listening comprehension and grammar learning compared with traditional focus on forms. The findings showed that dictogloss was more beneficial on both listening and grammar learning.

Idek and Fong (2015) examined the effectiveness of dictogloss in promoting L2 learners' learning of irregular verbs. The results of this study suggested that learners who were taught by the dictogloss outperformed learners in the other group who were instructed by the conventional grammar tasks (control group). Dictogloss can substitute drilling and memorizing exercises.

Overall, the main findings from empirical research on the possible effects of dictogloss indicate the following (see representative studies in Table 6):

· Dictogloss research showed mixed results when it is compared to other types of 'focus on form' (e.g. processing instruction, text reconstruction).
· Dictogloss is effective at promoting peer collaboration (Lim and Jacobs, 2001) and discussion (Nabei, 1996), and grammatical rules (Idek and Fong, 2015; HoKang, 2009).
· Dictogloss can be considered a multifunctional task which is beneficial in improving L2 learners' language skills and attention to form (García Mayo, 2002) in a meaningful context.

3.5.3 Structured Output

Structured output tasks are a meaningful focus-on-form type. These tasks carry a meaningful context and the target forms are produced not with the sole intention of practicing the target item, but rather to communicate opinions, beliefs, or other information related to designated topics.

The empirical research into the relative effects of structured output has mainly been conducted to address the following:

(a) Offline effects of structured output tasks compared to processing instruction
(b) Offline effects of structured output tasks compared to structured input

(a) Offline effects of structured output tasks compared to processing instruction

The effects of structured output tasks have been compared to processing instruction. The processing instruction group has been found to significantly outperform the structured output group on interpretation tasks on the English simple past tense (Benati, 2005); the Italian and French subjunctive (Lee and Benati, 2007a); the Spanish subjunctive (Farley, 2001a); and Spanish direct object pronouns (VanPatten, Farmer and Clardy, 2009). The interpretation scores of the two treatment groups have also been shown to improve equally on the Spanish subjunctive (Farley, 2001b; 2004) and Spanish direct object pronouns (Morgan-Short and Bowden, 2006). The results are mostly consistent for production measures, as L2 learners in both focus on form types improved

Table 6 Dictogloss representative studies

Study	Linguistic Feature/ Language	Subjects/L1	Treatments	Tests	Results
Lim and Jacobs (2001)	English dyadic verbal interaction	Chinese, Cantonese and Korean	Dictogloss	Interviews and questionnaires	Need for collaborative skills to be taught and for students to understand the value of cooperation
García Mayo (2002)	English third-personsingular-s-	Basque Spanish	CLIL Mainstream EFL	Dictogloss task	Results showed that CLIL learners noticed and produced more instances of the 3rd person singular -s than mainstream learners
VanPatten et al. (2009)	Object pronouns and word order in Spanish	English	Dictogloss Processing instruction Control	Interpretation	PI > DG
Idek and Fong (2015)	English irregular verbs	Malay	Dictogloss Control	Production Questionnaire	Dictogloss > Control

Note: I = Processing instruction; DG = Dictogloss

significantly and equally from pre-tests to post-tests (Benati, 2005; Farley, 2001a, 2001b, 2004; Lee and Benati, 2007a; Morgan-Short and Bowden, 2006; VanPatten, Farmer and Clardy, 2009). The findings of this line of investigations on the interpretation tasks are mixed. However, VanPatten, Farmer, and Clardy (2009) attributed the relative effects of structured output on interpretation tasks to the fact that in this group L2 learners could have been exposed to incidental structured input.

(b) Offline effects of structured output tasks compared to structured input

Despite the fact that there is a large number of studies (see Leeser, forthcoming and Shintani, 2014 for a meta-analysis of research on processing instruction) which have investigated the relative effects of structured output-based instruction versus processing instruction, there is a lacuna in the research body of evidence as far as investigating structured input versus other output-based pedagogical type of focus on form in isolation or combination. To address this gap, Benati and Batziou (2017, 2019) have recently explored discourse and long-term effects of structured input and structured output when delivered in isolation or in combination on the acquisition of the English causative. Greek learners of English participated in this study and were assigned to three groups: structured input only group; structured output only group; combined structured input and structured output group. The assessment tasks included an interpretation and production task at discourse-level. The results indicated that learners who received structured input both in isolation and in combination benefitted more than L2 learners who received structured output only. These two groups were able to retain instructional gains three weeks and six months after instruction in all assessment measures.

Overall, the main findings from empirical research on the possible effects of structured output indicate the following (see representative studies in Table 7):

· Structured input practice is the main component in processing instruction and should precede structured output practice.
· Structured input/processing instruction is overall superior to structured output/meaning output-based instruction to alter input processing problems and subsequently to have an impact on learners' developing system and what L2 learners can access under controlled and less controlled situations.
· Instruction should move from input (structured input) to output (structured output) to be effective in second language acquisition.

Table 7 Structured output representative studies

Study	Linguistic Feature/ Language	Subjects/ L1	Treatments	Tests	Results
VanPatten, Farmer and Clardy 2009	Spanish object pronouns	English	PI MOI	Interpretation and production at sentence-level	PI > MOI
Benati and Batziou (2017)	English causative forms	Greek	SI SI + SO SO	Interpretation and production at discourse-level	PI = SI + SO > SO (interpretation) PI = SI + SO > SO (production)

Note: PI = Processing instruction; C = Control; SI = Structured input; SO = Structured output; MOI = Meaning output-based instruction

3.6 What Are the Main Takeaways?

- Input flood might be effective in increasing L2 learners' explicit knowledge particularly when it is compared to explicit instruction. However, in terms of implicit knowledge, the studies investigating possible effects of input flood on implicit knowledge did not show any significant effects. The effectiveness of input flood might be related to factors such as the length of the treatment and the nature of the linguistic feature. Input flood might increase the chances that L2 learners might initially notice a specific target form in the input language they are exposed to, but noticing is not fully guaranteed.
- Input enhancement's main purpose is to draw L2 learners' attention to a specific form by increasing its visual saliency using typographical devices (e.g. increased size, different font, underlining, or embolding). The main purpose of this type of focus on form is to manipulate input to increase the chances for L2 learners to notice and then acquire the form incidentally. Overall, the empirical findings are mixed, indicating some positive effects on the learning of the forms under investigation. However, different researchers have come to different conclusions on the efficacy of input enhancement. A number of factors might constrain the effects of input enhancement on the acquisition of grammar: proficiency level, developmental stage and degree of readiness of the learner, type of linguistic feature chosen, and intensity of the treatment. It is important for findings on input enhancement and its role in awareness and attention to be confirmed in online studies employing a more fine-grained measure (i.e. eye tracking). Even if product-level tests fail to highlight new knowledge, eye movements measured at the process level in different studies show the effectiveness of textual enhancement in terms of amount of attention paid to target items.
- Processing instruction and, in particular, structured input activities are used to facilitate form–meaning connections among L2 learners. Processing instruction is an effective type of focus on form. Learners with different first languages (L1s) and backgrounds make consistent gains in interpretation and production tests at sentence- and discourse-level. The effects of processing instruction are consistent, durative, and measurable for different languages and processing problems. L2 learners who receive training in one type of processing strategy for one specific form transfer the use of that strategy to other forms without further instruction. Processing instruction and/or structured input alters the strategies that L2 learners use to process input in real time. Structured input activities have a measurable effect on L2 learners' moment-by-moment processing of input. This new line of enquiry (online testing) is currently limited to a few empirical studies, one principle,

a few target structures, four languages, and two online methods (self-paced tests and eye-tracking). This line of research (online) in processing instruction is very much in its infancy: It needs to be expanded to include a wider variety of input processing principles, L2s, target forms and structures, and online methods.

- Corrective feedback has been classified either as reformulation or as prompt type. There is a large database measuring the effects of corrective feedback. Overall, the results indicate the following: (i) feedback might be more effective by using additional intonational prompts; (ii) feedback is more effective when targeting a single linguistic feature at a time; (iii) the effects of feedback may not be immediate but gradual; (iv) it is useful to correct the same error on different occasions so that L2 learners can have enough exposure to the correct form; (v) not all grammar forms and structures respond equally to instruction and corrective feedback; (vi) L2 learners may notice lexical errors more effectively than morphosyntactic errors; (vii) feedback with uptake is more effective than feedback with no uptake; (viii) the acquisition of some grammatical structures may follow developmental sequences, meaning learners learn when they are developmentally ready; and (ix) for corrective feedback to be effective, teachers should match the feedback with learners' developmental stages.

- Consciousness-raising tasks require L2 learners to work collaboratively to complete a grammatical analysis of some kind which is either deductive or inductive in nature. The database is very small; however, this collaborative focus-on-form task is certainly effective in leading to interaction among L2 learners. Consciousness raising is better than traditional instruction and is an effective structured type of focus on form in developing explicit knowledge about a target form.

- Dictogloss is effective at developing language skills and at promoting interaction and learning explicit grammatical rules. Dictogloss is an effective text-reconstruction type of task.

- Structured output-based tasks seem to be effective when followed by structured input activities in helping L2 learners to make appropriate form–meaning connections at the interpretation level (both sentence and discourse) and produce sentences and discourse containing accurate forms.

4 What Are the Implications and New Avenues for Research?

4.1 What Are the Main Theoretical Implications?

Since Long's (1983) original paper on whether or not instruction makes a difference, empirical research and contemporary theories in second language acquisition have investigated and debated the role and nature of instruction. Overall, research findings seem to indicate that instruction on formal features of language does not affect order and sequence in language development. However, instruction on formal features of language might speed up the rate of acquisition under certain conditions. There are important factors (e.g. quality of input, type of focus on form) that might affect the effects of instruction and speed up acquisition of certain forms. We also need to consider the nature of language and the qualitative difference between explicit and implicit knowledge. Explicit rules cannot be equated to language which is an abstract, unconscious, and complex system. Language as mental representation is too abstract and complex to be taught and learnt explicitly. Mental representation bears no resemblance to what is traditionally taught and practiced. It builds up over time due to consistent and constant exposure to input data and interaction with universal properties of the language.

There is broad agreement among scholars in second language acquisition about the existence of two qualitatively different types of language knowledge: explicit/learned and implicit/acquired knowledge. There is also broad agreement that language acquisition is mainly implicit – meaning L2 learners can't articulate what is the content of language as mental representation – and in addition that grammatical rules found in textbooks, for example, do not constitute the basis for how language develops in learner's heads.

Explicit and implicit knowledge are qualitatively different. Explicit grammar rules might describe the language, but they do not correspond to the implicit representations the brain relies on for language development. To create an internal language system, L2 learners process streams of speech (VanPatten, Smith and Benati, 2019) and internal mechanisms build on this data to create an implicit system. While the priority of implicit over explicit knowledge is widely acknowledged, there is less agreement in relation to how it is achieved. The debate involves one central issue: can explicit knowledge influence the development of implicit knowledge? Some researchers believe that explicit knowledge can affect the development of the implicit system in some way. However, the mechanisms responsible for how these two systems might connect are not clear and the research measuring the effects of explicit instruction is biased towards the testing explicit knowledge.

From some of the studies reviewed in this Element measuring the effects of instruction (focus on form) we can certainly conclude that explicit learning affects the development of explicit knowledge. The points made here are fundamental in regard to the effectiveness of formal classroom instruction. Essentially, if explicit knowledge of rules cannot turn into the desired implicit knowledge, then traditional grammar instruction (focus on forms) is probably not an effective use of limited classroom time.

The main goal of language teaching should be the learner's acquisition of implicit knowledge as highlighted by Long (2017). Therefore, the key question is: Does focus on form or a particular type of focus on form facilitate and influence the development of implicit knowledge?

As reviewed in this Element, there is a large database of studies measuring the role and effects of focus on form on second language acquisition. The studies reviewed in this Element have generally the following methodological characteristics:

- They use a short-term research design measuring the effects of focus on form over a short period (immediately or after few weeks);
- They take place in a classroom with whole groups of students or in laboratories where participants receive individual treatment via computer-mediated instruction;
- They normally use a standard pre-/post-test design.

Overall the findings from research on focus on form indicate some beneficial effects for focus on form on the learning (mainly explicit) of the formal properties of the languages investigated. The main findings of processing instruction research also highlight the beneficial effects of this type of focus on form in helping learners to make appropriate form–meaning connections. Meta-analyses (e.g. Go et al., 2015; Norris and Ortega, 2000; Spada and Tomita, 2010) on the role and effects of instruction have overall concluded that instruction makes a difference. However, as pointed out by VanPatten, Smith, and Benati (2019: 118) a number of questions need to be addressed before we can be sure of these positive findings.

- What is it that the researcher is measuring? What does it mean to 'know' something? In particular, does the research on the effects of instruction measure explicit knowledge or implicit knowledge?
- What kind of task can be used to measure what learners know and how do we know it is a valid measurement?
- If we are looking at what learners can do after treatment, the same questions apply about what is measured and how it is measured.
- What is the nature of the treatment? What is it trying to affect? Does the treatment attempt to affect explicit knowledge or implicit knowledge (or something else)?
- How does the treatment reflect what we know about acquisition more generally and what does the researcher believe he or she is 'altering' in the learner? That is, what underlying 'processes' does the instruction attempt to affect?

Most of the studies in Norris and Ortega's (2000) meta-analysis, for example, used tests that mainly measured explicit knowledge. Measurements of implicit knowledge and in-depth language processing should be adopted by research measuring the effects of focus on form. There is a clear and overwhelming bias towards testing explicit knowledge in the research on the effects of focus on form. For now, the best conclusion about research on the effects of focus on form is this: instruction clearly helps explicit knowledge, at least in the short run. It is still not yet clear what it does, if anything, for implicit knowledge.

4.2 What Are the Main Pedagogical Implications?

Considering that language is complex, implicit and abstract, instruction should not consist of explanation of rules (paradigms) followed by mechanical practice (Benati, 2020). Traditional practice (focus on forms) might help to develop a language-like behaviour (skill) but it not responsible for language development (mental representation of language). Therefore, instruction should be less about the teaching of rules and more about exposure to form. There are types of 'focus on form' reviewed in this Element that can, in certain cases and conditions, enhance and speed up the way certain things are learned and can be an effective way to incorporate a focus on form component within an overall communicative approach to language pedagogy.

Focus on form comes in a variety of ways. Instructors are free to explore what pedagogical interventions might be a suitable and effective focus on form in the communicative language classroom. In their approach to focus on form, instructors should consider the following general guidelines:

- Ensure that L2 learners are exposed to language input that is manipulated (comprehensible and meaningful) so to facilitate language processing;
- Encourage L2 learners to make accurate form–meaning mappings;
- A focus on form should approach should consider both a focus on form and a focus on meaning at the same time;
- Input-based focus on form (e.g. textual enhancement, structured input) should perhaps precede out-based pedagogical interventions such as structured output tasks;
- Use a variety of focus on form types as one size does not fit all.

4.3 What Are the Main Avenues for Future Research on Focus on Form?

Classroom research investigating the effects of instruction is biased towards the testing of explicit knowledge. Future research would need to consider the following:

(i)　The nature and characteristics of implicit knowledge and how it can be measured;

(ii)　The use of appropriate pedagogical interventions (e.g. input and processing-based) that can have an effect on L2 learners' implicit knowledge system.

There is an overwhelming bias towards testing explicit knowledge in the research on the effects of instruction. The main finding of this research is that instruction makes a difference in traditional pencil-and-paper tests. Researchers must begin to measure implicit knowledge. Practitioners must ensure they foster the development of language in L2 learners and are not simply aiming at fostering a learning-like behaviour in L2 learners. Language instructors must use pedagogical interventions that facilitate language processing and the development of implicit knowledge.

Classroom research investigating the effects of instruction, must consider the use of online measurements. These methodological tools (self-paced listening and reading, eye-tracking, ERPs) might offer us the possibility of more fine-grained information and analysis about moment-by-moment sentence comprehension and can be a reliable measurement of implicit knowledge.

In terms of theory and research on language development, a clear distinction needs to be made between mental representation and skill in language development. Language is an implicit, abstract, and complex system and language development is input and input-processing dependent. At the same time, output processing is ordered and stage-like constrained. Therefore, any consideration in relation to the role of instruction in second language acquisition should account for these facts (Schwieter and Benati, 2019).

The research on focus on form has provided mixed results and the results of the research are not always clear. One of the problems with the research is the way scholars have been measuring outcomes of the pedagogical intervention under investigation. As previously argued, there is a certain bias towards explicit testing and tapping of explicit knowledge in the research on focus on form. Current empirical research on the effects of different types of focus on form clearly indicates that an element of instruction might be beneficial for language development. Traditional types of 'focus on forms' have been replaced by pedagogical interventions which present one form at a time in meaningful contexts designed to promote L2 learner noticing and processing of meaning–form connections. Some of the main conditions for acquisition of a grammatical form are: (a) noticing of target forms; (b) repeated meaningful exposure to input containing the form: (c) opportunities to make form–meaning connections; and (d) because the acquisition of grammar properties is affected by internal processing constraints and language development sequences, spontaneous and accurate production cannot be instantaneous and will naturally require time. Because of how language grows in the mind and communication develops over time, a meaningful approach to focus on form (one that moves from input to output) might facilitate the rate of acquisition.

Bibliography

On the Nature of Language

DeKeyser, R. (2015). Skill acquisition theory. In B. VanPatten & J. Williams (eds.), *Theories in second language acquisition*, 2nd ed. (94–112). New York: Routledge.

Housen, A., Kuiken, F. (2009). Complexity, accuracy and fluency in second language acquisition. Special issue. *Applied Linguistics*, 30 (4).

Keating, G. (2018). *Second language acquisition: The basics*. New York: Routledge.

VanPatten, B. (2010). Two faces of SLA: Mental representation and skill. *Journal of English Studies*, 10, 1–18.

VanPatten, B. (2016). Why explicit knowledge cannot turn into implicit knowledge. *Foreign Language Annals*, 49, 650–7.

VanPatten, B., Benati, A. (2010). *Key terms in second language acquisition*. London: Bloomsbury

VanPatten, B., Rothman, J. (2014). Against rules. In A. Benati, C. Laval & M. Arche (eds.), *The grammar dimension in instructed second language learning* (15–35). London: Bloomsbury.

On the Role of Instruction

Benati A. (2020). *Key questions in language teaching*. Cambridge: Cambridge University Press.

Krashen, S. (1982). *Principles and practice in second language acquisition*. London: Pergamon.

Ellis, N. C. (2012). Frequency-based accounts of SLA. In S. M. Gass and A. Mackey (eds.), *Handbook of second language acquisition* (93–210). New York: Routledge.

Goo, J., Granena, G., Yilmaz, Y., Novella, M. (2015). Implicit and explicit instruction in L2 learning: Norris and Ortega (2000) revisited and updated. In P. Rebuschat (ed.) *Implicit and explicit learning of languages* (443–482). Amsterdam: John Benjamins.

Kang, E., Sok, S., Han, ZhaoHong (2019). Thirty-five years of ISLA on form-focused instruction: A meta-analysis. *Language Teaching Research*, 23, 428–53.

Long, M. (1983). Does second language instruction make a difference? *TESOL Quarterly*, 17, 359–82.

Norris, J., Ortega, L. (2000). Effectiveness of second language instruction: A research synthesis and quantitative meta-analysis. *Language Learning*, *50*, 417–528.

Paradis, M. (2004). *A neurolinguistics theory of bilingualism*. Amsterdam: John Benjamin.

Pienemann, M., Lenzing, A. (2015). Processability theory. In B. VanPatten & J. Williams (eds.), *Theories in second language acquisition*, 2nd ed. (159–79). New York: Routledge.

Schmidt, R. (1995). Consciousness and foreign language learning: A tutorial on attention andawareness in learning. In R. Schmidt (ed.), *Attention and awareness in foreign language learning* (1–63). Honolulu: University of Hawai'i Press.

Schwieter, J., Benati, A. (2019). *The Cambridge handbook of language learning*. Cambridge: Cambridge University Press.

Spada, N., Tomita, Y. (2010). Interactions between type of instruction and type of language feature: A meta-analysis. *Language Learning*, *60*, 263–308.

VanPatten, B., Smith, M., Benati, A., (2019). *Key questions in second language acquisition: An introduction*. Cambridge: Cambridge University Press.

Wong, W., Simard, D. (2018). *Focusing on form in language instruction*. New York: Routledge.

On the Nature of Focus on Form

Benati, A. (2013). *Key issues in second language teaching*. London: Equinox.

Benati, A., Schwieter, J. (2019). Pedagogical interventions to L2 grammar instruction. In J. Schwieter & A. Benati (ed.), *The Cambridge handbook of language learning* (475–99). Cambridge: Cambridge University Press.

Doughty, C., Williams, J. (eds.). (1998). *Focus-on-form in classroom second language acquisition*. Cambridge: Cambridge University Press.

Ellis, R. (2016). Focus on form: A critical review. *Language Teaching Research*, 20, 405–28.

Long, M. (1991). Focus on form: A design feature in language teaching methodology. In K. de Bot, R. Ginsberg & C. Kramsch (eds.), *Foreign language research in cross-cultural perspective* (39–52). Amsterdam: John Benjamins.

Long, M. (2015). *Second language acquisition and task-based language teaching*. Malden, MA: Wiley Blackwell.

Long, M. (2017). Instructed second language acquisition (ISLA): Geopolitics, methodological issues, and some major research questions. *Instructed Second Language Acquisition* 1, 7–44.

Long, M., Robinson, P. (1998). Focus on form: Theory, research and practice. In C. Doughty, & J. Williams (eds.), *Focus on form in classroom second language acquisition* (15–41). Cambridge: Cambridge University Press.

Nassaji, H., Fotos, S. (2011). *Teaching grammar in second language classrooms*. New York: Routledge.

Ranta, L., Lyster, R. (2017). Form-focused instruction. In P. Garrett & J. Cots (ed.), *The Routledge handbook of language awareness* (40–56). New York: Routledge.

On the Effects of Focus on Form

Input Enhancement

Alanen, R. (1995). Input enhancement and rule presentation in second language acquisition. In R. Schmidt (ed.), *Attention and awareness in foreign language learning* (259–302). Honolulu: University of Hawai'i Press.

Alsadoon, R. (2015). Textual input enhancement for vowel blindness: A study with Arabic ESL learners. *The Modern Language Journal*, 99, 57–79.

Boers, F., Demecheleer, M., He, L., Deconinck, J., Stengers, H., Eyckmans, J. (2017). Typographic enhancement of multiword units in second language text. *Language Learning*, 27, 448–69.

Choi, S. (2016). Processing and learning of enhanced English collocations: An eye movement study. *Language Teaching Research*, 21, 403–26.

Cintrón-Valentín, M., Ellis, N. (2015). Exploring the interface: Explicit focus-on-form instruction and learned attentional biases in L2 Latin. *Studies in Second Language Acquisition*, 37, 197–235.

Doughty, C. (1991). Second language acquisition does make a difference: Evidence from an empirical study of SL relativization. *Studies in Second Language Acquisition*, 13, 431–69.

Hernàndez, T. (2011). Reexamining the role of explicit instruction and input flood on the acquisition of Spanish discourse markers. *Language Teaching Research*, 15, 159–82.

Indrarathne, B., Kormos, J. (2016). The role of working memory in processing input: Insights from eye-tracking. *Bilingualism: Language and Cognition*, 21, 355–74.

Issa, B., Morgan-Short, K., Villegas, B., Raney, G. (2015). An eye-tracking study on the role of attention and its relationship with motivation. *EUROSLA Yearbook*, 15, 114–42.

Izumi, S. (2002). Output, input enhancement, and the noticing hypothesis: An experimental study on ESL relativization. *Studies in Second Language Acquisition*, 24, 541–77.

Jourdenais, R., Ota, M., Stauffer, S., Boyson, B., Doughty, C. (1995). Does textual enhancement promote noticing? A think aloud protocol analysis. In R. Schmidt (ed.), *Attention and awareness in foreign language learning* (183–216). Honolulu: University of Hawaii Press.

LaBrozzi, R. (2014). The effects of textual enhancement type on L2 form recognition and reading comprehension in Spanish. *Language Teaching Research*, 20, 75–91.

Lee, M., Révész, A. (2020). Promoting grammatical development through captions and textual enhancement in multimodal input-based tasks. *Studies in Second Language Acquisition*, 42, 625–51.

Lee, S-K. (2007). Effects of textual enhancement and topic familiarity on Korean EFL students' reading comprehension and learning of passive. *Language Learning*, 57, 87–118.

Lee, S.-K., Huang, H. (2008). Visual input enhancement and grammar learning: A meta-analytic review. *Studies in Second Language Acquisition*, 30, 307–31.

Leow, R. (1997). The effects of input enhancement and text length on adult L2 readers' comprehension and intake in second language acquisition. *Applied Language Learning*, 8, 151–182.

Leow, R. (2001). Do learners notice enhanced forms while interacting with the L2? An online and offline study of the role of written input enhancement in L2 reading. *Hispania*, 84, 496–509.

Leow, R., Egi, T., Nuevo, A., Tsai, Y. (2003). The roles of textual enhancement and type of linguistic item in adult L2 learners' comprehension and intake. *Applied Language Learning*, 13, 1–16.

Meguro, Y. (2017). Textual enhancement, grammar learning, reading comprehension, and tag questions. *Language Teaching Research*, 23, 58–77.

Overstreet, M. (1998). Text enhancement and content familiarity: The focus of learner attention. *Spanish Applied Linguistics*, 2, 229–58.

Rahimi, S., Ahmadian, M., Amerian, M., Dowlatabadi, H. R. (2020). Comparing accuracy and durability effects of jigsaw versus input flood tasks on the recognition of regular past tense /-ed/. *Open Sage*.

Reinders, H., Ellis, R. (2009). The effects of two types of input on intake and the acquisition of implicit and explicit knowledge. In R. Ellis, S. Loewen, C. Elder, R. Erlam, J. Philp, & R. Reinders (eds.), *Implicit and explicit knowledge in second language learning, testing and teaching* (282–302). Bristol: Multilingual Matters.

Sharwood Smith, M. (1993). Input enhancement in instructed SLA: Theoretical bases. *Studies in Second Language Acquisition*, *15*, 165–79.

Shook, D. J. (1994). What foreign language reading recalls reveal about the input-to-intake phenomenon. *Applied Language Learning*, 10, 39–76.

Simard, D. (2009). Differential effects of textual enhancement formats on intake. *System*, 37, 124–35.

Simard, D., Fortier, V., Foucambert, D. (2013). Measuring metasyntactic ability among heritage language children. *Bilingualism: Language and Cognition*, 16, 19–31.

Szudarski, P., Carter, R. (2016). The role of input flood and input enhancement in EFL learners' acquisition of collocations. *International Journal of Applied Linguistics*, 26, 245–65.

Toomer, M., Elgort, I. (2019). The development of implicit and explicit knowledge of collocations: A conceptual replication and extension of Sonbul and Schmitt (2013). *Language Learning*, 69, 405–39.

Trahey, M., White, L. (1993).Positive evidence and preemption in the second language classroom. *Studies in Second Language Acquisition*, 15, 181–204.

White, J. (1998). Getting the learners' attention: A typographical input enhancement study. In C. Doughty & J. Williams (eds.), *Focus on form in classroom second language acquisition* (85–113). Cambridge, MA: Cambridge University Press.

Williams, J., & Evans, J. (1998). What kind of focus and on which forms? In C. Doughty & J. Williams (eds.), *Focus on form in classroom second language acquisition* (139–55). Cambridge, MA: Cambridge University Press.

Winke, P. (2013). The effects of input enhancement on grammar learning and comprehension. A modified replication of Lee (2007) with eye-movement data. *Studies in Second Language Acquisition*, 35, 323–52.

Wong, W. (2002). Modality and attention to meaning and form in the input. *Studies in Second Language Acquisition*, 23, 345–368.

Wong, W. (2005). Input enhancement: From theory and research to the classroom. New York: McGraw-Hill.

Zyzik, E., Marqués Pascual, L. (2012). Spanish differential object marking: An empirical study of implicit and explicit instruction. Studies in Hispanic and Lusophone Linguistics, 12, 387–422.

Processing instruction

Benati, a. (2004a). the effects of structured input and explicit information on the acquisition of italian future tense. In b. vanpatten (ed.), processing instruction: theory, research, and commentary (207–55). mahwah, nj: erlbaum.

Benati, A. (2004b). The effects of processing instruction and its components on the acquisition of gender agreement in Italian. *Language Awareness*, 13, 67–80.

Benati, A. (2005). The effects of processing instruction, traditional instruction and meaning-output instruction on the acquisition of the English past simple tense. *Language Teaching Research*, 9, 87–113.

Benati, A. (2013a). The input processing theory. In P. Garcia Mayo (ed.), *Contemporary approaches to second language acquisition* (93–110). Amsterdam: John Benjamins.

Benati, A. (2013b). Age and the effects of processing instruction on the acquisition of EnglishPassive constructions among school children and adult native speakers of Turkish. In J. F. Lee & A. Benati (eds.), *Individual differences and processing instruction* (83–104). Sheffield, UK: Equinox.

Benati, A. (2019). Classroom-oriented research: Processing instruction. *Language Teaching.* 52,3, 343–59.

Benati, A. (2020). The effects of structured input and traditional instruction on the acquisition of the English causative passive forms: An eye-tracking study measuring accuracy in responses and processing patterns. (forthcoming in *Language Teaching Research*).

Benati, A. (forthcoming). *Input processing and processing instruction: The acquisition of Italian and Modern Standard Arabic.* Amsterdam: Benjamins Publishing.

Benati, A., Lee, J. (2008). *Grammar acquisition and processing instruction.* Clevedon: Multilingual Matters.

Benati, A., Lee, J. (2010). *Processing instruction and discourse.* London: Bloomsbury.

Benati, A. G., Lee, J. F. (eds.). (2015). Processing instruction: New insights after twenty years of theory, research and application [Special issue]. *IRAL*, 53.

Benati, A., Batziou M. (2017) The effects of structured-input and structured-output tasks on the acquisition of English causative. *IRAL*, 57, 265–288.

Benati, A., Batziou M. (2019) Discourse and long-term effects of structured-input and structured-output tasks in combination and isolation on the acquisition of passive English causative forms. Accepted and forthcoming in *Language Awareness*, 28, 1–18.

Benati, A., Schwieter, J. (2017). Input processing and processing instruction: Pedagogical and cognitive considerations for L3 acquisition In A. Tanja & A. Hahn (eds.), *L3 Syntactic Transfer: Models, New Developments and Implications* (195–223). Amsterdam: John Benjamins.

Chiucchiu, G., Benati, A. (2020). The effects of structured input and textual enhancement on the acquisition of Italian Subjunctive: A self-paced reading study. Forthcoming in *Instructed Second Language Acquisition*.

Farley, A. (2001a). The effects of processing instruction and meaning-based output instruction. *Spanish Applied Linguistics*, 5, 57–94.

Farley, A. (2001b). Authentic processing instruction and the Spanish subjunctive. Hispania, 84, 289–99.

Farley, A. (2004). Processing instruction and the Spanish subjunctive: Is explicit information needed? In B. VanPatten (ed.), *Processing instruction: Theory, research, and commentary* (227–39). Mahwah, NJ: Erlbaum.

Henry, N. (2015). Morphosyntactic processing, cue interaction, and the effects of instruction: An investigation of processing instruction and the acquisition of case markings in L2 German (Unpublished doctoral dissertation)

Ito, K., Wong, W. (2019). Processing instruction and the effects of input modality and voice familiarity on the acquisition of the French causative construction. *Studies in Second Language Acquisition*, 41, 443–68.

Lee, J. (2015). The milestones in twenty years of processing instruction research. *International Review of Applied Linguistics in Language Teaching*, 53, 111–26.

Lee, J., VanPatten, B. (2003). *Making communicative teaching happen*, 2nd ed. New York: McGraw-Hill.

Lee, J., Benati, A. (2007a). *Delivering processing instruction in classrooms and virtual contexts*. London: Equinox.

Lee, J., Benati, A. (2007b). *Second language processing: An analysis of theory, problems and possible solutions*. Continuum: London

Lee, J., Benati, A. (2009). *Research and perspectives on processing instruction*. Berlin: Mouton de Gruyter.

Lee J., Doherty, S. (2018), Native and nonnative processing of active and passive sentence: The effects of processing instruction on the allocation of visual attention. *Studies in Second Language Acquisition*, 41, 1–27.

Morgan-Short, K., Bowden, H. (2006). Processing instruction and meaningful output-based instruction: Effects on second language development. *Studies in Second Language Acquisition*, 28, 31–65.

VanPatten, B. (1996). *Input processing and grammar instruction: Theory and research*. Norwood, NJ: Ablex.

VanPatten, B. (2015a). Input processing in adult SLA. In B. VanPatten and J. Williams (eds.), *Theories in second language acquisition* (113–35). New York: Routledge.

VanPatten, B. (2015b). Foundations of processing instruction. *IRAL*, 53, 91–109.

VanPatten, B., Cadierno, T. (1993). Explicit instruction and input processing. *Studies in Second Language Acquisition*, 15, 225–43.

VanPatten, B., Fernández, C. (2004) The long-term effects of processing instruction. In B. VanPatten (ed.), *Processing instruction: Theory, research, and commentary* (273–289). Mahwah, NJ: Erlbaum.

VanPatten, B., Oikkenon, S. (1996). Explanation vs. structured input in processing instruction. *Studies in Second Language Acquisition*, 18, 495–510.

VanPatten, B., Wong, W. (2004). Processing instruction and the French causative: Another replication. In B. VanPatten (ed.), *Processing instruction: Theory, research, and commentary* (97–118). Mahwah, NJ: Erlbaum.

VanPatten, B., J. Farmer., C. Clardy. (2009). Processing instruction and meaning- based output instruction: A response to Keating and Farley (2008). *Hispania*, 92, 116–26.

Wong, W., Ito, K. (2018). The effects of processing instruction and traditional instruction on L2 online processing of the causative construction in French: An eye-tracking study. *Studies in Second Language Acquisition* 40, 241–68.

Interactional and corrective feedback

Ammar, A., Spada, N. (2006) One size fits all? Recasts, prompts and L2 learning. *Studies in Second Language Acquisition*, 28, 543–574.

Carpenter, H., Jeon, K. S., MacGregor, D., Mackey, A. (2006). Learners' interpretations of recasts. *Studies in Second Language Acquisition*, *28*, 209–236.

Doughty, C., Varela, E. (1998) Communicative focus on form. In C. Doughty and J. Williams (eds.), *Focus on form in classroom second language acquisition.* (114–38). Cambridge: Cambridge University Press.

Ellis, R., Loewen, S., Erlam, R. (2006). Implicit and explicit corrective feedback and the acquisition of L2 grammar. *Studies in Second Language Acquisition* 28, 339–69.

Egi, T. (2007). Recasts, learners' perceptions, and L2 development. In A. Mackey (ed.), *Conversational interaction in second language acquisition: A series of empirical studies* (249–67). Oxford: Oxford University Press.

Ellis, R. (2012) *Language teaching research and language pedagogy.* Oxford: Wiley-Blackwell.

Gass, S., Mackey, A. (2015). Input, interaction and output in second language acquisition. In B. VanPatten & J. Williams (eds.), *Theories in second language acquisition: An introduction* (175–199). Mahwah, NJ: Lawrence Erlbaum Associates.

Go, J., Mackey, A. (2013). The case against the case against recasts. *Studies in Second Language Acquistion*, 35, 127–65.

Granena, G., Yilmaz, Y. (2019). Corrective feedback and the role of implicit sequence-learning ability in L2 online performance. *Language Learning*, 69, 127–56.

Han, Z. H. (2002). A study of the impact of recasts on tense consistency in L2 output. *TESOL Quarterly*, 36, 543–72.

Lightbown, P., Spada, N. (1993). *How languages are learned*. Oxford: Oxford University Press.

Lyster, R. (1998). Recasts, repetition, and ambiguity in L2 classroom discourse. *Studies in Second Language Acquisition* 20, 51–81.

Lyster, R. (2004) Differential effects of prompts and recasts in form-focused instruction. *Studies in Second Language Acquisition*, 26, 399–432.

Lyster, R., Izquierdo, J. (2009). Prompts versus recasts in dyadic interaction. *Language Learning* 59, 453–98.

Lyster, R., Ranta, L. (1997) Corrective feedback and learner uptake: Negotiation of form in communicative classrooms. *Studies in Second Language Acquisition*, 19, 37–66.

Lyster, R., Saito, K. (2010). Oral feedback in classroom SLA: A meta-analysis. *Studies in Second Language Acquisition* 32.2, 265–302.

Lyster, R., Saito, K., Sato, M. (2013) Oral corrective feedback in second language classrooms. *Language Teaching*, 46(1), 1–40.

Loewen, S., Philp, J. (2006). Recasts in the Adult English L2 classroom: Characteristics, explicitness, and effectiveness. *Modern Language Journal*, 90, 536–56.

Mackey, A., Philp, J. (1998). Conversational interaction and second language development: Recasts, responses, and red herrings? *The Modern Language Journal* 82, 338–356.

Nabei, T., Swain, M. (2002). Learner awareness of recasts in classroom interaction: A case study of an adult EFL student's second language learning. *Language Awareness* 11, 43–63.

Nassaji, H. (2009). Effects of recasts and elicitations in dyadic interaction and the role of feedback explicitness. *Language Learning* 59, 411–52.

Nassaji, H. (2017). The effectiveness of extensive versus intensive recasts for learning L2 grammar. *Modern Language Journal* 101.2, 353–68.

Panova, I., Lyster, R. (2002). Patterns of corrective feedback and uptake in an adult ESL classroom. *TESOL Quarterly* 36, 573–95.

Ranta, L., Lyster, R. (2007) A cognitive approach to improving immersion students' oral language abilities: The Awareness-Practice-Feedback sequence. In R. DeKeyser (ed.), *Practice in a second language: Perspectives from applied linguistics and cognitive psychology* (141–60). Cambridge: Cambridge University Press.

Rassaei, E. (2020). The separate and combined effects of recasts and textual enhancement as two focus on form techniques on L2 development. *System*, 89, 1–14.

Sato, M. (2013). Beliefs about peer interaction and peer corrective feedback: Efficacy of classroom intervention. *The Modern Language Journal* 97, 611–33.

Saito, K., Lyster, R. (2012) Effects of form–focused instruction and corrective feedback on L2 pronunciation development of /r/ by Japanese learners of English. *Language Learning*, 62(2), 595–33.

Sheen, Y. (2007) The effects of corrective feedback, language aptitude, and learner attitudes on the acquisition of English articles. In A. Mackey (ed.), *Conversational interaction in second language acquisition: A collection of empirical studies*. (301–22). Oxford: Oxford University Press.

Yang, Y., Lyster, R. (2010). Effects of form-focused practice and feedback on Chinese EFL learners' acquisition of regular and irregular past tense forms. *Studies in Second Language Acquisition* 32, 235–63.

Output and collaborative focus on form tasks

Alegría de la Colina, A., García Mayo, M. P. (2007). Attention to form across collaborative tasks by low-proficiency learners in an EFL setting. In M. P. García Mayo (ed.), *Investigating Tasks in Formal Language Settings* (91–116). Clevedon: Multilingual Matters.

Basterrechea, M., García Mayo, M. P. (2013). Language-related episodes (LREs) during collaborative tasks: A comparison of CLIL and EFL learners. In K. McDonough & A. Mackey (eds.), *Second language interaction in diverse educational contexts* (25–43). Amsterdam: John Benjamins.

Basterrechea, M., García Mayo, M. P., Leeser, M. J. (2014). Pushed output and noticing in a dictogloss: task implementation in the CLIL classroom. *Porta Linguarum*, 22, 7–22.

Ellis, R. (1987). Interlanguage variability in narrative discourse: Style shifting in the use of the past tense. *Studies in Second Language Acquisition*, 9, 1–19.

Fotos, S. (1994) Integrating grammar instruction and communicative language use through grammar consciousness-raising tasks. *TESOL Quarterly*, 28, 323–51.

Fotos, S., Ellis, R. (1991) Communicating about grammar: A task-based approach. *TESOL Quarterly*, 25, 605–28.

HoKang, D. (2009). The role of DG on both listening and grammar. *English Education Journal*, 5(2), 1–23.

Idek, S., Fong, L. L. (2015). The use of DG as an information gap task in exploiting dual application principle in learning irregular verbs. *Journal of Management Research, 7*(2), 481.

Kuiken, F., Vedder, I. (2002). The effect of interaction in acquiring the grammar of a second language. *International Journal of Educational Research, 37* (3–4), 343–58.

Leeser, M. J. (2004). Learner proficiency and focus on form during collaborative dialogue. *Language Teaching Research, 8*(1), 55–81.

Leeser, M. (Forthcoming). A research synthesis and meta-analysis of processing instruction.

Lim, W. L., Jacobs, G. M. (2001). An analysis of students' dyadic interaction on a dictogloss task. ERIC Document Reproduction Service No. ED 456 649.

García Mayo, M. P. (2002). The Activeness of Two Form-Focus Tasks in Advanced EFL Pedagogy. *International Journal of Applied Linguistic, 12*, 156–75.

Mehnert, U. (1998). The effects of different lengths of time for planning on second language performance. *Studies in Second Language Acquisition, 20*, 83–108.

Nabei, T. (1996). DG: Is it an effective language learning task? *Working Papers in Educational Linguistics, 12*, 59–74.

Qin, J. (2008) The effect of processing instruction and dictogloss tasks on acquisition of the English passive. *Language Teaching Research, 12*, 61–82.

Rutherford, K. (2001). An investigation of the effects of planning on oral production in a second language. (Unpublished MA thesis.) University of Auckland.

Swain, M., Lapkin, S. (2001). Focus on form through collaborative dialogue: Exploring task effects. In M. Bygate, P. Skehan & M. Swain (eds.), *Researching pedagogic tasks* (56–89). London: Longman, Pearson Education.

Shintani, N. (2014) The effectiveness of Processing Instruction and production-based instruction on L2 grammar acquisition: A meta-analysis. *Applied Linguistics, 36*, 306–25.

Smart, J. (2014) The role of guided induction in paper-based data-driven learning. *ReCALL, 26*, 184–201.

Sugiharto, S. (2006). Grammar consciousness raising: Rresearch, theory and application. *Indonesian JELT, 2*, 16–23.

VanPatten, B., Inclezan, D., Salazar, H., Farley, A. (2009). Processing instruction and dictogloss: A study on object pronouns and word order in Spanish. *Foreign Language Annals, 42*, 557–75.

Wajnryb, R. (1990). *Research books for teachers: Grammar dictation*: Oxford: Oxford University Press.

Yeo, K. (2002). The effects of DG: A technique of focus on form. *English Teaching*, 57, 149–67.

Yip, V. (1994). Grammatical consciousness-raising and learnability. In T. Odlin (ed.), *Perspective on pedagogical grammar* (123–39). Cambridge: Cambridge University Press

Acknowledgements

I would like to express my gratitude to the University of Hong Kong for providing me with the necessary support to complete this element. A special thanks to the anonymous reviewers and for their valuable and priceless feedback on the first draft of this element.

Cambridge Elements ≡

Second Language Acquisition

Alessandro Benati

The University of Hong Kong

Alessandro Benati is Director of CAES at The University of Hong Kong (HKU). He is known for his work in second language acquisition and second language teaching. He has published groundbreaking research on the pedagogical framework called Processing Instruction. He is co-editor of a new online series for Cambridge University Press, a member of the REF Panel 2021, and Honorary Professor at York St John University.

John W. Schwieter

Wilfrid Laurier University, Ontario

John W. Schwieter is Associate Professor of Spanish and Linguistics, and Faculty of Arts Teaching Scholar, at Wilfrid Laurier University. His research interests include psycholinguistic and neurolinguistic approaches to multilingualism and language acquisition; second language teaching and learning; translation and cognition; and language, culture, and society.

About the Series

Second Language Acquisition showcases a high-quality set of updatable, concise works that address how learners come to internalize the linguistic system of another language and how they make use of that linguistic system. Contributions reflect the interdisciplinary nature of the field, drawing on theories, hypotheses, and frameworks from education, linguistics, psychology, and neurology, among other disciplines. Each Element in this series addresses several important questions: What are the key concepts?; What are the main branches of research?; What are the implications for SLA?; What are the implications for pedagogy?; What are the new avenues for research?; and What are the key readings?

Cambridge Elements ☰

Second Language Acquisition